THE FESTIVAL SHAKESPEARE

Love's Labor's Lost

THE FESTIVAL SHAKESPEARE

Love's Labor's Lost

The New York Shakespeare Festival Series

Bernard Beckerman and Joseph Papp, Editors

With an essay on the direction of the play
by GERALD FREEDMAN

THE MACMILLAN COMPANY, NEW YORK

COLLIER-MACMILLAN LIMITED, LONDON

Library of Congress Catalog Card Number: 68-20763

First Printing

The Macmillan Company, New York

Collier-Macmillan Canada Ltd., Toronto, Ontario

PRINTED IN THE UNITED STATES OF AMERICA

Contents

Contents

Preface to the New York Shakespeare Festival Series

Every presentation of a Shakespearean play is a unique event in a continuing tradition. The event is unique because each production must confront a play as though it had never been staged. A theatrical company, as it were, must "forget" that it is presenting a play written by Shakespeare before it can tap the full power of his imagination. And yet, each production is still but one in the continuing tradition of exploring the seemingly infinite prospects of Shakespeare's world. In the crucible of rehearsal each cast rediscovers the play, adding its own sensibilities to the accumulated vision of the work.

The present series is a record of such rediscoveries by the New York Shakespeare Festival. It consists of separate volumes of Shakespeare's plays produced by the Festival. A historical introduction provides the critical and theatrical background against which the director's statement can be viewed. Throughout the series stress has been placed on each director's statement, for in each case it reflects the outlook that guided the production. Photographs and production notes offer specific illustrations of the manner in which the director's approach received concrete expression. A complete text of the play, conveniently marked to indicate stage cuts, enables the reader to compare the full copy with the

performed copy. Though each volume reflects the concerns of a particular production, yet taken together, the
series conveys the spirit animating the New York
Shakespeare Festival as a whole.

From its beginnings in 1953, when it was founded
by Joseph Papp, the guiding policy of the Festival has
been to provide a theater for all regardless of ability to
pay. During the summer of 1956 the Shakespeare Workshop, as the forerunner of the Festival was then called,
presented its first season of Free-Shakespeare-in-the-Park
at the East River Amphitheater in lower Manhattan.
In 1957, the summer season opened at Belvedere Lake
in Central Park, continued with a tour of the five bor-
oughs, and when the truck carrying stage and company
broke down, terminated in Central Park. For a time in
1959 the principle of free performances appeared to be
in jeopardy. The then Parks Commissioner insisted that
if performances were to be given in the park, admission
must be charged. However, after a series of legal con-
tests, the Appellate Court upheld the Shakespeare
Workshop, and the way was paved for the expansion
of the Festival.

In 1959 the Board of Estimate of the City of New
York appropriated funds for the construction of a permanent amphitheatre at Belvedere Lake. These funds
proving insufficient, they were supplemented by George
T. Delacorte. Stability was further assured when in 1960
the Board of Regents of the State of New York granted
an absolute charter to the newly named New York
Shakespeare Festival. Finally, on June 19, 1962, a new
summer season opened the 2,300-seat Delacorte Theater
with a production of *The Merchant of Venice*.

At the same time as it consolidated its position in
the center of Manhattan, the Festival extended its influence throughout the rest of the city. Commencing in

1960, the Board of Education underwrote annual tours of the New York City schools by one of the Festival productions. In 1964 the Festival initiated summer tours of city parks and playgrounds by a mobile unit. To reach a still broader segment of the population, the tours included plays in Spanish as well as in English. At last, in 1966, with the acquisition of the former Astor Library as a permanent home and indoor theater, the New York Shakespeare Festival established itself on a year-round-production basis.

The Festival itself is in the tradition of the folk or popular theater of Europe. The right of attendance by all citizens is unequivocally established, and so the audiences represent a cross-section of the urban populace. The integrity of production is maintained, and therefore the plays are presented without condescension. The premise is that the best of drama can be communicated clearly and effectively as spontaneous experience, not archaic curiosity. Perhaps it is not sheer coincidence that the Delacorte Theater has many features in common with Shakespeare's Globe: its open stage, its unroofed amphitheater, its ample capacity. Nor may it be coincidence that the Festival relies so much on touring, just as Shakespeare and his fellows did. Both the structure of the theater and the practice of touring may be essential conditions for the vigorous interplay between citizenry and performer so necessary to a healthy theater and so integral to the purposes of the New York Shakespeare Festival.

The Editors

The History of the Play

✍ *by Bernard Beckerman*

Slender in plot, courtly in manner, affected in poetic diction, *Love's Labor's Lost*, it had been long thought, was a work of Shakespeare's apprenticeship, which perhaps held special interest for his own age but attracted few admirers in the years that followed. Neither stage nor study housed it sympathetically, and as recently as the turn of this century, George C. Odell, writing about Shakespearean production from Betterton to Irving, could see no reason for reviving the play. Yet, with the revolution of Shakespearean production initiated by William Poel at the end of the nineteenth century, and with the expansion of marathon festivals in the twentieth, it was inevitable that even such a slightly regarded play would be presented. To the amazed delight of critics and audiences, repeated viewings have increasingly revealed the merits of the comedy. As one Shakespearean editor, J. Dover Wilson, confessed, the artistry of the play was not evident until it emerged in production. More than most of Shakespeare's works, *Love's Labor's Lost* requires theatrical exposure in order to release its distinctive charm and appeal.

In its own day the play commanded a measure of popularity. Notice of it first appeared in 1598. Sometime during that year, Cuthbert Burby issued a quarto of the play, on the title page of which appeared a refer-

ence to a performance before Queen Elizabeth "this
last Christmas," probably the Christmas of 1597. Sometime after September 7, but before the end of 1598,
Palladis Tamia by Francis Meres was published. Match-
ing the ancient poets with his fellow Englishmen, poem
for poem, play for play, Meres finds that they do not
suffer unduly by comparison. "As Plautus [is] accounted
the best for Comedy . . . among the Latines: so Shakespeare among the English . . . For Comedy, witnes . . .
his Loue Labors Lost." A more personal effect of Shakespeare's pen is reflected in a poem by Robert Tofte,
dated in the same year:

> Loves Labour Lost, I once did see a Play
>   Yclepéd so, so calléd to my paine,
> Which I to heare to my small Joy did stay,
>   Giving attendance on my froward Dame,
>   My misgiving minde presaging to me Ill,
>   Yet was I drawne to see it against my will.
>
> Each Actor played in cunning wise his part,
>   But chiefly Those entrapt in Cupids snare:
> Yet all was feignéd, 'twas not from the heart,
>   They seemed to grieve, but yet they felt no care:
>   'Twas I that Griefe (indeed) did beare in brest.
>   The others did but make a show in Jest.

Poor Tofte! In the title of his poem, *Alba, or the
Months Mind of a Melancholy Lover* (1598) he echoes
the sentiments, if not the words, of *Love's Labor's Lost*.
Such a confluence of allusion to one of Shakespeare's
plays in one year is not usual and attests, in some degree
at least, to the impact made on London by this play.

But though these references fix the terminal date for
Love's Labor's Lost, they do not enable us to determine
how long before 1598 the play was composed. Tofte

The Festival Shakespeare *Love's Labor's Lost*
states that he "once did see" the play, but whether
"once" implies once long ago, or only one performance,
is not positive. The full title of the 1598 quarto is
equally ambiguous. It reads:

> A/ PLEASANT/ Conceited Comedie/ CALLED,/ Loues
> labors lost./ As it was presented before her Highnes/
> this last Christmas./ Newly corrected and aug-
> mented/ By W. *Shakespere*/ Imprinted at London
> by W.W./ for *Cuthbert Burby*./ 1598.

Again it is not clear to what the phrase "newly corrected and augmented" refers. Does it mean that the
play had been revised and enlarged prior to publication?
Or does it mean that this printing of 1598, in contrast
to an earlier inferior version, was the authentic copy? In
1599 Burby issued a quarto edition of *Romeo and Juliet*,
"newly corrected, augmented, and amended," to replace
the bad quarto of 1597. By analogy we might suppose,
as scholars generally do, that the 1598 Quarto of *Love's
Labor's Lost* was also issued to replace a defective copy,
and that the statement on its title page, like the one
on the title page of the 1599 Quarto of *Romeo and
Juliet*, was inserted to advise the prospective reader that
he was receiving the full and correct text.

Evidently such caution became advisable by this date.
The 1598 quarto of *Love's Labor's Lost* was the first
publication to credit Shakespeare with authorship from
its initial printing. In the same year the second editions
of *Richard II* and *Richard III* added the name of Shakespeare as author, whereas the first editions had omitted
it from the title pages. Apparently, by 1598 Shakespeare's name on a publication had commercial value,
inducing, in one instant at least, sharp practice by
William Jaggard. In 1599 Jaggard published a collection of poems entitled A *Passionate Pilgrim*, which he

attributed to Shakespeare though, as examination shows, the collection contains work by Barnfield, Deloney, possibly Marlowe and others, as well as by Shakespeare. Among the selections are three from *Love's Labor's Lost*. They are the love poems written by Don Armado, Longaville, and Dumaine.

Recently J. W. Lever has shown that the play, at least in its quarto state, could not have been completed before 1597. For those entranced by the image of Shakespeare as nature's poet, it may be disillusioning to discover that the dramatist did not always draw his details of life from his own observation. Not the meadow but Gerard's *Herball*, according to Lever, suggested the "lady smocks" and "cuckoobuds" of the final song in *Love's Labor's Lost* (V. ii. 884–885). Since Gerard's book was first registered in June 1597, it is unlikely that Shakespeare could have seen a copy before the summer or fall of that year. Presumably then, the present text of *Love's Labor's Lost* was completed between the end of spring and the performance of the play during the Christmas season.

That the play was originally written in 1597 is hardly likely. Too many factors point to the probability that the play was written some years earlier. The description of the 1598 quarto as a "corrected and augmented" edition is one piece of evidence. Another is the considerable degree of reiteration that can be found throughout the text. A curious feature of the script, not present to this extent in any other copy of a Shakespearean play, is the appearance of two versions of the same speeches within a scene. Berowne's apostrophe to the academy of women's eyes (IV. iii. 284–360), his first exchanges with Rosaline (II. i. 113–126, 178–192), and Berowne's plea for service and Rosaline's grim rejoinder (V. ii. 807–812, 827–844) are examples. To consider only the first instance, compare lines 291–312 and lines 313–349 of Act IV, scene iii. The subject matter in both sections is identical. Even phrases are repeated. Early in his speech, Berowne avers that

> From women's eyes this doctrine I derive:
> They are the ground, the books, the academes,
> From whence doth spring the true Promethean fire.
>
> (297–299)

Later he repeats the idea in a slightly different sequence.

> From women's eyes this doctrine I derive.
> They sparkle still the right Promethean fire;
> They are the books, the arts, the academes,
> That show, contain, and nourish all the world;
>
> (345–348)

It is self-evident that here we have two treatments of one motif.

Several explanations for this repetition have been suggested. Initially in 1923 and again in 1962, J. D. Wilson argued that each passage represented a distinct version of the play. In his view Shakespeare wrote *Love's Labor's Lost* sometime before 1597. The first part of Berowne's speech (291–312) belongs to that earlier writing. Then in 1597 Shakespeare came to rewrite the play, at which time he revised Berowne's speech (313–348). By chance both versions were preserved in the author's manuscript. This explanation was rejected by W. W. Greg and E. K. Chambers. Sifting the various pieces of textual and structural evidence amassed by Wilson, neither could see why the discrepencies could not be explained by a single writing of the play. As Chambers reasoned, "The [alternate] passages can be just as well interpreted as false starts at the time of the original writing." In the main this position was defensible until Lever demonstrated Shakespeare's reliance on Gerard. Since then it has become apparent that unless we are prepared to date the initial writing in 1597, either Wilson's explanation of revision must stand or another one must be supplied. The newest theory has been proffered by G. Lambrechts. He argues that the disputed passages embody the original text by Shakespeare and an abridgment by another hand. Such a theory is not without merit, but until it is more substantially developed, the best explanation is still the supposition that Shakespeare wrote the play before 1597 and revised it in that year.

When he did the original writing and under what circumstances remains a mystery. At one time the fashion was to regard the play as one of the first, if not *the* first dramatic work by Shakespeare. F. G. Fleay conceived of elaborate metrical tests to demonstrate how the poetry observed a structural regularity, which, he argued, showed the hand of the novice. This test merely systematized an impression shared by such authorities as Halliwell-Phillipps and Coleridge. To them the affected style and simplicity of plotting suggested a youthful hand. More recently Alfred Harbage has reaffirmed the arguments for considering *Love's Labor's Lost* a very early work. In his introduction to the Pelican edition, Harbage points out the affinities between Lyly's comedies, written for performance by a children's company, and this play by Shakespeare, and urges consideration of the possibility that "Shakespeare wrote the play for Paul's [a children's troupe] in 1588–89 and salvaged it as a novelty for his own company in 1596–97." Such a possibility is reinforced by historical allusions contained in the text. An embassy by Marguerite of Valois to her estranged husband, Henry King of Navarre, occurred at Nerac in 1578. This event may very well have served as the immediate source of the play. If it is the source, Harbage argues, it would more likely have been put to dramatic use in the late 1580's than in 1593, when Henry's conversion to Catholicism made Navarre a distasteful name in England.

While recognizing that Marguerite's embassy might indeed be a source for *Love's Labor's Lost,* J. D. Wilson and Richard David, in their editions, emphasize the cumulative verbal parallels and character allusions that link the play to the literary war between Thomas Nashe and Gabriel Harvey, the titles of whose pamphlets, *Pierce Penilesse his Supplication to the Divell* (1592) and *Pierce's Supererogation* (1593) respectively, were echoed in the bantering on purses and piercing (IV. ii.). And in Moth, that "tender Juvenal," they follow Fleay in seeing the image of Nashe. They also argue that *Love's Labor's Lost* shares the lyricism of the non-dramatic poetry Shakespeare was composing at the time, specifically the sonnets and *Venus and Adonis.* Perhaps the simplicity of the plot of *Love's Labor's Lost* is attributable to Shakespeare's infatuation with such lyricism at this date. The very formality of the versification —telling evidence of early writing, according to Fleay— may just as easily be seen as illustration of a sophisticated and matured style of expression. However artificial the play might seem, it balances neatly the pretensions of refinement against the natural touches of unaffected thought and action. Such a balance argues mastery rather than apprenticeship so that insofar as style is at issue, the play can be dated in Shakespeare's lyrical period of 1593–94.

Because of the rarified atmosphere of the play, critics tend to regard *Love's Labor Lost* as a "coterie" drama intended for an exclusive audience and written for private showing. Wilson conjectures that it was first performed at the Earl of Southampton's home at Christmas 1593. Of course, such conjecturing is not confined to this play alone. Lists of noble weddings and royal entertainments have been combed to find the occasions when *A Midsummer Night's Dream* and *The Merry Wives of Windsor* as well as *Love's Labor's Lost* were first presented, and though in each instance investigation has been thorough, it has not achieved any reliable results. In all likelihood we shall never know whether *Love's Labor's Lost* was first shown in a private palace to an aristocratic audience or in a public playhouse to a hodgepodge London gathering. But if we cannot ascertain the specific facts, we can at least consider the general practice of theatrical production and thus understand what may have happened.

Rarely, if ever, during the last half of the sixteenth century, was a play especially commissioned for an aristocratic celebration. When the Queen or the nobility desired a presentation for a particular occasion, they usually commissioned a masque or an allegorical display. Plays for the most part were products of commercial enterprise. They were sold by free-lance writers to one of the London companies or, as in the case of Shakespeare, were specifically written for one company.

A new play was presented as soon as it was completed by the dramatist. Invariably the first performance was in the public playhouse before a paying audience. If and when a troupe was summoned to Court, it would offer one of its more recent productions for the entertainment of the Queen. Such was the sequence, we may suppose, that was followed in the presentation of *Love's Labor's Lost*.

Sometime in 1593 Shakespeare completed the comedy. That he may have based it on an earlier play is altogether possible, as it was not uncommon for one

author to revise the play of another. Presumably the
Lord Chamberlain's men, the company to which Shakespeare belonged, presented the work without delay. In
the normal rhythm of the Elizabethan repertory system,
the play may have received ten to twenty performances
over the next year or two, only to fade gradually from
the stage. Then in 1597, whether for public performance or in anticipation of the Christmas season held at
Court, the play was revived. Though not every revival
involved the rewriting of a script, many plays did un-
dergo various degrees of contraction or expansion at the
time they were revived. For instance, in 1599 *Old
Fortunatus* was considerably rewritten for public presentation, and within a month rewritten once more, though
slightly, for the private presentation that followed at
Court. Perhaps the revision of *Love's Labor's Lost* in
1597 was also for public performance, since there is no
sign of address to the Queen, nor any other expression
of devotion to a royal or noble audience. Shortly after
the 1597 performance before the Queen, *Love's Labor's
Lost* was published.

Admittedly, this foregoing history, though probable,
is hypothetical. Not hypothetical, however, were exactly
similar circumstances that followed. Apparently the popularity of *Love's Labor's Lost* continued, for in 1605,
nearly ten years later, the play was revived again, much
in the fashion described. As a letter from Sir Walter
Cope to Robert Cecil testifies, Shakespeare's fellows,
by then entitled the King's men, "have revived an old
[play] called *Love's Labor's Lost*." That they did not
revive it specifically for the Court is clear, because Cope
recommends the play as a last resort. It is the only one,
not already seen by Queen Anne, that the players can
perform immediately. In order to assure Cecil that the
play is suitable, Cope describes it as one "which for wit

and mirth [Richard Burbage, the actor] says will please [the Queen] exceedingly." It appears that Burbage's word was accepted, for Court records confirm performance of the comedy that Christmas season.

For the next eighteen years the record is dark; then *Love's Labor's Lost* appears in the folio collection of Shakespeare's works (1623). The text of this edition is virtually the same as it was in 1598, for the copy used in printing was based on the quarto. Whatever variations crept into the folio text were minor and, insofar as scholars can determine, did not stem from independent authority. As for the play's fortunes in the playhouse after 1605, little is known. The comedy seems to have enjoyed continuing favor. In 1631 a second quarto was printed. Its title page cites performances at both the Globe and Blackfriars, the indoor theater operated by the King's men. Thus, despite its evident topicality, the play seems to have been performed into the 1630's.

Later years, however, did not prove quite so kind. It would be another two hundred years and more before the play returned to the stage. Throughout the Restoration and eighteenth century, *Love's Labor's Lost* was considered at best an uneven play and at worst, as Collier expresses the matter in 1699, "a very silly one." In 1672 John Dryden dismissed the play along with *The Winter's Tale*, *Pericles*, and *Measure for Measure* as "grounded on impossibilities, or at least so meanly written, that the comedy neither caused . . . mirth, nor the serious part . . . concernment." In 1710 Charles Gildon, the actor, termed *Love's Labor's Lost* "one of the worst of Shakespeare's plays, nay I think I may say the very worst." The play has the dubious distinction of being the only Shakespearean work not performed during the eighteenth century. Even the attempt to adapt Shakespeare was a failure in this case. Whereas "improved"

versions of *Lear* and *Romeo and Juliet* flourished
throughout the eighteenth century, *The Students*—"A
Comedy Altered from Shakespeare's Love's Labour's
Lost, and Adapted to the Stage"—seemed never to have
been actually presented. Its publication in 1762 served
neither the vanity of its author, whoever he may have
been, nor the cause of this "pleasant conceited" comedy,
which continued to be regarded as an inferior expression
of Shakespeare's genius.

Perhaps Samuel Johnson best and most generously
gives a balanced estimate of the play during this period.

> In all this play, which all the editors have concurred
> to censure, and some have rejected as unworthy of
> our Poet, it must be confessed that there are many
> passages mean, childish, and vulgar. . . . But there are
> scattered, through the whole, many sparks of genius.

In Johnson the balance is struck against the play. By
1817 William Hazlitt, weighing the merits and demerits
of *Love's Labor's Lost*, is inclined to conclude somewhat more in favor of the play. On one hand, if he
were obliged "to part with any of [Shakespeare's] . . .
comedies," this is the first he would discard. But then
he bethinks him of Don Armado and the other creatures of Shakespeare's fancy and gradually becomes rec-
onciled to the whole for the sake of its parts. In the
same year Coleridge is won over too, not by the characters, but by "the intellectual action" of the play. His
admiration is for the activity of mind, for the way in
which Shakespeare conveys "profound truths in the
most lively images."

That neither critic could quite shake off his unhap-
piness about the comedy is reflected in a curious point
each adopted in a slightly different way. Coleridge and
Hazlitt both suggest that Shakespeare aped the English

court of his day, and as Hazlitt puts it, did so "too
Faithfully." A later echo of this view is sounded by
W. W. Lloyd in Singer's edition of Shakespeare (1856),
who remarks that the play "reflects the age too truth-
fully." Essentially the argument is that by imitating the
affectation of his society too well, Shakespeare con-
stricted his work, depriving it of any interest for succeed-
ing generations. Thus, refusing to fault the dramatist,
the commentators found fault with his subject. Commencing with these critics, the balance begins to shift.
Gradually, the imperfections of the comedy recede into
the background, the excellencies become more promi-
nent. As so often occurs in the criticism of the lesser
plays, a change of taste is heralded by a German writer.
As early as 1847 the critic and philosopher Ulrici could
describe *Love's Labor's Lost* as a "graceful play," one
that captures "the significant contrast between the fresh
reality of life which ever renews its youth, and the
abstract, dry, and dead, study of philosophy." There is
a deeper side to the comedy, but "this deeper signifi-
cance of the merry piece, with its fine irony and harm-
less satire is, of course, not expressed in didactic breadth,
but only intimated in a playful manner." The unre-
served admiration by Ulrici is not echoed by either
English or German critics for nearly half a century. Not
until Walter Pater's appreciation of the play appeared
in the December 1885 number of *Macmillan's Magazine*
did an English critic express unqualified praise of *Love's
Labor's Lost*. What distinguishes his essay is the fact
that, while he recognized the peculiarly Elizabethan
character of the play, he treats that character as equally
appealing to his taste and the taste of his readers. He
conveys an immediate response to the play without the
intermediary of intellectual or historical justifications.
The exquisiteness and refinement of Berowne's sensi-

bility attract Pater's fancies. In Berowne he finds something of Shakespeare himself, and though normally such
biographical criticism is irrelevant and misleading, in
this instance Pater's awareness of Shakespeare in the
person of Berowne enhances an appreciation of the play.

By the time Pater came to praise *Love's Labor's Lost*,
it had already arisen from the page like a phoenix. In
1839 Madame Vestris in association with Charles James
Matthews selected the play for revival on the occasion
of their assuming management of Covent Garden.
Handsomely mounted, with the settings "from the prac-
ticed pencil of the Grieves," master scene painters of
dazzling spectacle, the play returned to the stage on
September 30, 1839. Unfortunately, the premiere was
marred by a riot when the management closed off the
shilling gallery. Whether the effects of the riot or the
reportedly miserable acting defeated the first revival in
two hundred years, the production continued for a mere
run of nine performances and then was discontinued.

Eighteen years later, to the day, Samuel Phelps revived the play, this time at Sadler's Wells. Though
somewhat more successful than the Vestris revival, this
production did not stimulate imitators at once. The
first Stratford Memorial Theatre production of the play
occurred in 1885 when, reportedly, Phelps' prompt book
was employed. In 1893 William Poel supervised an
open reading of the play, for which Swinburne congrat-
ulated him warmly. That presentations in the nineteenth
century were limited to so few reflects the coolness with
which revivals of the play were received.

The first producer in the United States to become
enamored of the play was Augustin Daly. He presented
the initial American performance on February 21, 1874
at the Fifth Avenue Theatre. On March 28, 1891 he
revived the play at Daly's Theatre with Ada Rehan and

John Drew. The version he employed was rather heavily cut, especially in the Armado-Moth sequences. For instance, Armado and Moth's meeting with Costard (III. i. 1–133) was reduced from one hundred and thirty-three lines to thirty-nine, and Berowne's rhapsody on the pedagogical efficacy of love (IV. iii. 284–360), from seventy-six lines to thirty-two. In this type of excision Daly was merely following widespread practice. The Vestris revival had also used a severely curtailed text, for it was not until the twentieth century that uncut or nearly uncut versions of the play reached the stage.

During this entire period, and continuing through the first two decades of the twentieth century, the revivals were largely fitful. Nowhere did the play win firm popular response. Beginning in 1919, however, a series of revivals in England culminated with popular and artistic success in the nineteen-forties. Between 1919 and 1932 six productions or readings of the play were offered by English repertory theaters, such as Sir Barry Jackson's Birmingham Repertory, or by amateur societies. In 1932 Tyrone Guthrie, taking over the direction from the ailing Ernest Milton, staged an elegant version of *Love's Labor's Lost* at the Westminster Theatre, a version full of rhythm and headlong spirit, sometimes sacrificing sense in his pursuit of the music, it was charged. It was this production that was instrumental in taking Guthrie to the Old Vic. It was also instrumental in winning admirers for the play. Several other productions followed in the thirties, including another by Guthrie in 1936. But it was not until the Peter Brook production of 1946 at Stratford and the Hugh Hunt production of 1949 at the New Theatre that the comedy achieved broad acceptance. Excellent casts, the former headed by Paul Scofield, the latter by

Michael Redgrave, were able to achieve the grace, the wit, and the dash calculated to elicit ungrudging admiration.

In the United States the play languished for more than half a century after Daly's production of 1891. Not until 1951 was *Love's Labor's Lost* revived by the Brattle Theatre in Cambridge, Massachusetts. Updating the period of the play, the director, Albert Marre, set the events in an Edwardian England. Ferdinand became a country gentleman, and his academe, a country estate. Arrival of the ladies by motorcar and a match at croquet enlivened the proceedings. Familiarity in this instance bred critical success. Early in 1953 the production was revived at the New York City Center, where it enjoyed a limited, though respectable run.

This gradual acclimation of the play to the modern theater preceded a much slower reconsideration of the play in the library. For one thing critics were loathe to give the work serious attention. Even in a book devoted solely to Shakespearean comedy, published in 1938, H. B. Charlton did not deign to include the play in the substance of his study. Instead he relegated discussion of it to a few pages of summary. For him, as for so many other scholars, interest in the play was purely biographical. "Assuredly," Charlton wrote, it is Shakespeare's "least substantial comedy," a judgment unshaken until recently.

Whatever attention was expended on the play was directed principally toward regularizing the text and, more fully, toward uncovering the historical figures behind the comic characters. The satiric tone of *Love's Labor's Lost* has long been recognized. The game has been to discover the objects of satire. Warburton was the first to discern the person of John Florio, translator and teacher of Italian, behind the role of Holofernes the Pedant (1747). His assumption was challenged by Samuel Johnson, dismissed for a time, and in recent years, once again investigated seriously. Meanwhile, scholars have suggested other candidates for Holofernes as well as for Moth, Armado, and Nathaniel. Besides Nashe and Harvey, the candidates have included Sir Walter Raleigh and Thomas Harriot, the mathematician. In fact it has been this literary detective work, rather than dramatic criticism, which has excited the most lively interest about this play in scholarly circles. Until now, however, despite the avid interest and painstaking research, no one has yet succeeded in showing an indisputable connection between any fictional and actual person. In the absence of such conclusive connections, a more general relationship between the play and the period has been supposed. Much has been made of the so-called "school of night" (see IV. iii. 250) as the central object of Shakespeare's mockery, though it is still moot whether or not a band of intellectual nonconformists consisting of Raleigh, Harriot, Chapman, Northumberland, and others ever did exist. Oscar James Campbell may be correct, after all, that Shakespeare's satire was of a universal type, directed at no particular individual or group, owing more to the conventional figures of Italian comedy than to actual personages of the Elizabethan social scene.

By contrast with historical detective work, dramatic criticism has been scant. Two essays, one by Harley Granville-Barker, the other by E. M. W. Tillyard, at either end of a forty year span, best epitomize the growing appreciation of the comic richness and humane sensibility inhering in the artificiality of academic Navarre. Perhaps more than any other single stimulus, Granville-Barker's chapter on *Love's Labor's Lost* in his *Prefaces to Shakespeare* set the tone for the Guthrie revivals of

the thirties. Writing in 1927, Granville-Barker sketched
how the difficulties of the text could be surmounted in
production. He perceived that the potential enchant-
ment of the comedy lay in its vivacity. "There is life
in it," he asserted. But it requires that an actor's vitality
be brought to the "beauties of fancy and phrase" with
which the scenes abound. Mere resurrection of a youthful curiosity would not do. Animation of character
assisted by judicious excision, he was convinced, could
bring out the charm of the work.

Through his influence on theatrical production,
Granville-Barker helped to alter the literary estimate of
Love's Labor's Lost. In an essay on the comedy issued
in the same year that he completed his revised edition
(1962), J. D. Wilson tells the "story of [his] conversion" from skepticism about the play's virtues to un-
abashed admiration. Conversion was partly stimulated
by Granville-Barker's essay but fully brought about by
Guthrie's production, which gave him a new play "the
existence of which I had never suspected." The match-
ing of high spirits and pattern-playing revealed theatrical
values that removed any doubts of the play's delight-
fulness.

Perhaps because of happy productions, perhaps because of a general reaction against realism, *Love's
Labor's Lost* enjoys a higher reputation today than it
has ever had since its own day. Reluctant admirers,
the Hazlitts of the past, have yielded to wholehearted
advocates, such as Wilson and E. M. W. Tillyard. In
Shakespeare's Early Comedies (1965), Tillyard justifies
the play not merely in theatrical but also in human
terms. For him the play illustrates, in a playful yet
serious manner, the education of youth and the growth
of sensibility. It is not the elegance and artifice that
dominate the spirit of the play, but the common dis-

covery of folly and error, a discovery that heightens rather than dampens the natural ebullience of young men on the threshold of life.

Tillyard's interpretation finds a sympathetic echo in the New York Shakespeare Festival production. As the director's statement shows, the production of the play was not undertaken apologetically. There is no suggestion, as in Granville-Barker's preface, that the director thought he was dealing with a lesser work. He expresses a positive attitude, which it has taken more than three hundred years to fashion. *Love's Labor's Lost*, whatever topicalities it may have originally embraced, is now recognized as a vivid portrait of human types, most touched with a bit of pomposity, none without a trace of wisdom, all capable of learning to face the darkness of the world-outside-of-academe.

Directing *Love's Labor's Lost*

✑ *by Gerald Freedman*

The key to *Love's Labor's Lost* can be found in the final scene of the play, which begins with news of the death of the King of France. The change in mood is so sudden, the news itself so shocking, that it almost seems inappropriate coming as it does after the frivolous fun that has preceded and following the most outrageous and farcical scene in the play.

At first glance one might say, "Shakespeare was mistaken. This is no way to end a comedy." And indeed, the scene is often treated as if Shakespeare were mistaken.

What then is the reason for this seemingly abrupt appendage to a seemingly slick and fashionable comedy of manners? The scene, rather than being an embarrassing intrusion, is a testament to Shakespeare's genius as a writer for the theater. What to a reader of the play may seem clumsy, abrupt, or in bad taste, or what does not fit in conveniently with some preconceived intellectual pattern, works beautifully on stage, the place for which the scene was, after all, meant.

In *Love's Labor's Lost* Shakespeare has taken a common and rather superficial play form of the period and transcended its confines by infusing the material with his overflowing humanity and his knowledge of the mutability of human affairs. Throughout the play we find him filling out conventional characters of the period so they can no longer be neatly categorized.

What greater dramatic impact can the fateful news of the King's death have than coming as it does at the height of everyone's enjoyment, at a time when such news is least expected and most unwanted? And how must this change one's previous conception of *Love's Labor's Lost* as an artificial comedy? For most definitely it is not. It is a play filled with human feeling. It would be a mistake to let the artifice of the language or the apparent symmetry of the construction fool one. That final scene, which seems to upset the symmetry, which seems so offensive to the texture that came before it, is the moment toward which Shakespeare has been heading from the opening of the play. And on that fact, above all others, the director's artistic choices must be based.

Although at first I labeled the play, "The Game of Love," I realized soon enough that as a theme such a label could not encompass the final scene. In that scene the characters are not involved in playing a game. They are absolutely in earnest. The play, then, must be about something more than the superficial aspects of love, which "game" seems to imply: It must be about the truth of love between man and woman. The distinction between "the game of love" and "the truth of love" became my guiding thesis when I began rehearsals. I understood I was not dealing with characters who were merely social clotheshorses upon whom I would hang pretty lines and stagy gimmicks. I was dealing with full people—people vulnerable to chance, to pain, and, ultimately, to death.

I recall one production that was updated to some-

thing resembling Edwardian times. The production
attempted to deal with the play's genuine humor and
humanity by avoiding it, by substituting sight gags and
anachronisms for understanding. The final scene seemed
superfluous and intrusive because the audience had not
been prepared to accept any moment of reality or seriousness on the part of these characters. If Shakespeare
had intended us only to be faintly amused, he would
certainly have provided us with another ending, such as
he did in *The Comedy of Errors* and *The Taming of the
Shrew*. However, even in those plays, one finds that
special humor and humanity that sets Shakespeare apart
from other playwrights.

In approaching a comedy like *Love's Labor's Lost*, the
question of how to discover its style arises. As far as I
am concerned, the best way to approach style is not
to approach it at all. By that I mean, the best way to
achieve a play's style is to achieve it honestly, from the
bottom up, from the heart out, not to superimpose it,
not to apply it like varnish. I wanted to approach this
play naturalistically, to give the actors a very firm base
upon which to work, develop, and operate.

Actors have to deal with something in which they
can believe. They have to deal with many ideas, objects,
and people. They have to suggest various levels of commitment. They have to move with inner logic. They
cannot be made to do things simply because they fit a
certain style. If their behavior is truthful to the action
of a scene and to the play as a whole, and if this truth
is applied as well to all aspects of the production, a style
for the play will emerge.

Shakespeare's genius guides the actor to this truth.
His genius lies in his understanding of human nature
and his ability to take a contemporary and conventional

form of his theater and amplify it, embellish it, imbue it with such life, such reality, that in this case without sacrificing any of the various levels of humor, he enhances it all and lovingly suffuses it with a humanizing element. This is what has kept his works universal long after his contemporaries' plays of similar nature have simply disappeared, because they no longer mean anything to us, and their characters have become mere mouthpieces of a verbal language that has lost its power to communicate. Shakespeare, first and foremost, communicates in a human language of relationship and experience. This was the guideline in approaching the characters, and it was from this that the style of the production developed.

While actually directing the play, my early suppositions about *Love's Labor's Lost* were frequently discarded. For instance, on first reading I tended to see Navarre and the Princess as colorless cardboard figures. The only characters who seemed to come alive, aside from Don Armado and Costard, were Berowne and Rosaline. But actually, there is life throughout the whole course of the play, particularly if one realizes that characters do not have to be talking to make their presence felt. Shakespeare does not always give many lines to characterize a role, but he always gives important clues that make a role alive and vital to the fabric of the play.

In fact, in this production King Ferdinand and the Princess of France emerged as the two most important protagonists. This was not because Berowne and Rosaline, who are commonly thought of as the primary protagonists, were lesser actors (which they were not), but because the actors who performed the roles of the King and Princess understood and were able to communicate the dual quality of royal personages: the public image and the private emotions. Navarre and the Princess perform ceremony; they never truly forget the dignity and seriousness of their offices, but they are also human, youthful, whimsical, and susceptible to love. Certainly today, when newspapers and magazines keep us constantly informed of the "goings on" of royal couples, we need no longer fear to present kings and queens as full-bodied emotional creatures. Whatever else Navarre and the Princess may be, they are above all human beings.

Shakespeare presents them to us in their private world, accompanied by friends and confidants. There is nobody closer to Navarre than Berowne, Longaville, and Dumaine. It is quite possible that they were raised and educated together, and that they have been constant companions since childhood. And there is no one closer to the Princess than Rosaline, Katharine, and Maria. I tried to evolve a feeling of intimacy and familiarity among the young men and women. This meant a conscious working to create an ensemble effort. It meant casting all the roles as strongly as possible. Berowne and Rosaline were not to be treated as star parts. The flavor of the play is that of a chamber group. It has the qualities of Mozart's *Così fan tutte*—a glittering work of virtuosity for everyone. And when played as an ensemble, *Love's Labor's Lost* works magnificently. It becomes a beautifully attuned string orchestra, in which each player takes his cue from the other.

In approaching the body of this essay, I have detailed a scene by scene analysis of my approach to the problems presented in performing *Love's Labor's Lost* today. I am first concerned with the discovery and understanding of the "life" of the characters and the play beneath the surface of words and form. My second concern is the uncovering and application of the play's manifest humor for a contemporary audience.

THE PLAY

The opening stage direction reads, "Enter Ferdinand King of Navarre, Berowne, Longaville, and Dumaine." At once the King reminds his friends that he is going to turn the court into a small academy for the "Still and contemplative in living art" (14). My first thought was, why didn't he talk to them offstage? Why did he wait until this moment to make his speech? That led me to the assumption that the characters probably did not enter together, that the stage direction was only meant to indicate that now the actors were on stage and the dialogue was beginning.

My method as a director is to try to find out the logic behind human behavior. Therefore, it was necessary to discover the reason behind the King's opening speech. What precipitated its sudden release from thought? What makes Navarre speak now, at this moment, rather than at some other time?

In order to understand the King's edict, his wish to live the life of a scholar and an ascetic, I felt it necessary to show what came before; that is, in order to understand the life that is to be, I wanted first to show the life that already was. This I accomplished by seeking out those recreations that occupied the young men of the time. I especially wanted to discover those diversions that were both active and sensuous, that were not only particular to the young men of the Elizabethan court, but to the young men of any age.

I finally decided to begin the play with an informal sporting event, specifically with a game of badminton. What I wanted was a traveling entrance, one that could

begin offstage, involve the actors physically, and create
an atmosphere that was light and bouncy in keeping
with the spirit of the play. (Another consideration was
that in the Delacorte, as in most outdoor theaters, one
somehow has to establish the beginning of a play without opening a curtain. Doing so is always a problem, but
it is also a stimulant.) I was not interested in establishing a competitive contest, but rather a game of fun.
Hitting a shuttlecock back and forth seemed an ideal
choice. It would be at once active and arresting. I did
not want to assault the audience right at the beginning
with language, which in *Love's Labor's Lost* is often
complex and artificial, but to draw them into the action
by means of their other senses.

The task was set for the three men—Berowne,
Longaville, and Dumaine—to keep the shuttlecock in
the air, to have fun, to create an atmosphere of physical
liveliness. Immediately after the three men entered, I
had their servants follow with preparations for an elaborate picnic, another pleasurable and sensuous diversion.
I set the scene in an open garden court, a place that
was airy and free of political ceremony. In the center
of the set was a fountain, adorned with a romantic
nude female figure. The servants spread luxurious and
comfortable pillows about, placed a lovely picnic cloth
on the ground, brought in choice fruits and food and
drink—in every way sought to satisfy the demands of
their rich, spoiled, educated, and charming masters.

Then I had King Ferdinand enter on the upper land-
ing as if he had been offstage working on his severe
code of ethics. I felt it was important that he should
be separated from the activities of his companions,
inasmuch as he begins by reprimanding them and reminding them of their promise. It was right, too, that
he should be above them, as he is their king. He over-

sees them and examines their behavior, which he now finds reprehensible. Again, the physical action—that is, the King, who is separate and above—reinforces the intent of the scene.

One aspect of my directing in Central Park has been to stage the plays as if the members of the audience could not hear, but could only understand the action by what they saw. This is in no way meant to negate the importance of language, but is partly a response to the enormity of the outdoor space at the Delacorte Theater and partly an effort to encompass an audience that ranges from a highly literate group of people, who are very familiar with the literature and background of the plays, to those in our audience who do not even understand English, or who have a very limited use of the language and a very limited knowledge of the play.

The entire first scene is one of exposition. It is an extremely important scene, setting up as it does almost everything that is to follow. The challenge for the director is to make the scene interesting, to make the situation and the characters come to life, to explore the basic motives and conflicts so that the concern of the audience is aroused as the exposition is being delivered.

Although the opening lines indicate that there has been some prior discussion of the present edict, the fact that the young men must swear again led me to believe that the oath had not been taken seriously, and that Ferdinand, by necessity, had to use this moment to reinsure what had probably been agreed to in jest.

I had Navarre closely observe Berowne, Dumaine, and Longaville partaking of their pleasures before reminding them of their promise. He asks them to sign a paper which will confirm their oath that for three years' time they will live with him and keep his statutes. I had him

signal the servants to remove the picnic cloth, the food,
the badminton rackets—everything, in fact, that represented the life of ease and pleasure. Even the nude
statue was carried off and replaced with a telescope.
(The choice of the telescope stemmed from the recur-
ring image of light in the play, of seeing as knowledge,
and of the eyes as the instrument of seeing [see I. i.
42–45, 75–90; IV. iii. 218–228, 293–348].)

With proper handling, the opening scene almost immediately becomes a scene of drama, of conflicting ideas
and characters. The King has made a request of his
companions, and they have been reluctant to comply
with it. Now Navarre has to be stronger. He has to
adopt a strict and disapproving tone and exert his authority to bring his companions back into line.

Each of the young men is obliged to swear a new
oath and inscribe his name. During this pledge of alle-
giance, the young revelers reveal something about their
characters. Longaville uses the image of food in his oath.
Dumaine talks about manners and outward show. Both
their speeches are prim and proper. Berowne, however,
is something else. He immediately sets himself apart
from his friends. In contrast to them he is a breaker of
images. He is outspoken and adopts the pose of a cynic,
although one must see it as just that—a pose. For
beneath this armor of cynicism beats the heart of a
romantic.

Berowne's speech implies that the King has set up a
way of life that is more than slightly ridiculous; it is
impossible, against the laws of nature. To live by a
code of behavior that demands such excessive restraint
and asceticism is unnatural. Berowne, with wild exaggeration, tries to show his friends what they are up
against, hoping that by so doing they will see the foolishness of their vows. However, he has no intention of

going his own way. He knows that once he has accepted
a responsibility he is committed to it. He ridicules the
King's edict for its severity, but he knows that in the
end he will agree to abide by it.

When the King says, "Well, sit you out" (110),
Berowne quickly changes gears. His feeling of fellowship suppresses his awareness of the folly set before him.
No matter what, he prefers to be one of the boys. This
is part of the whole youthful feeling about the play, the
feeling of games and camaraderie, first among the men,
and later, games and camaraderie of a different sort,
among the men and women.

Berowne calls back his friends and reads through the
proclamation. The audience learns how excessive both
the code and the punishments are. No woman shall
come within a mile of the court, the penalty being to
lose her tongue; and no man shall talk to a woman
within the term of three years. Berowne, upon hearing
the sentence, ridicules Navarre for forgetting his diplomatic duty, which requires that the King honor the
presence of the recently arrived Princess of France. So
at the very height of the men's resolution, the rug is
pulled out from under their feet and a mirthful expectation of what is to follow is set up.

Navarre realizes that the Princess "must lie here on
mere necessity" (145), and Berowne, never passing up
an opportunity to use his wit, seizes the phrase and
turns it back on the King. "Necessity will make us all
forsworn/ Three thousand times within this three years'
space:/ . . ./ If I break faith, this *word** shall speak
for me,/ I am forsworn 'on mere necessity' " (146 ff.).

I did not have to look far for a modern equivalent to
the spirit of this play. The principal men reminded me

---

* Italics in the speeches cited are inserted by the author.

of very bright Harvard and Yale boys—impressive backgrounds, lots of education, and a slight thirst for the best that life has to offer. The young men in the play are sixteenth-century playboys, full of wit, wordplay, and fun. But they are also intelligent men, sincere men, men with feelings, and men who are open to learning.

The course of my direction thus far has been to set the tone of the play, establish the relationships, and define the characters. Navarre has something emotional to fight for, something that obviously means a great deal to him. He wants to prove that the intellect can keep the appetites in abeyance, that man can dominate his passions with his will. Berowne knows this is a foolhardy supposition, but so as not to break with his comrades, he acquiesces. He accepts the King's edict, which soon enough will meet with all sorts of difficulties.

Costard's entrance (177) gives a new impulse to the first scene and thrusts the low comedy elements smack into the body of the main action, with the character of Dull officiously and aggressively propelling Costard into the scene by the scruff of his leather jerkin. Costard is the con man who always finds a way to turn a situation to his advantage, managing to sneak through life, enjoying himself, without any great responsibility or commitment to anyone.

Since I always look for what is happening in a scene and not necessarily what the scene says, I asked myself, "What is Costard doing in this first scene?" Whether Costard is working in terms of physical movement or ideas, his aim is "to get out" of trouble, "to get out" of a compromising situation, "to get out" of the law's hands. Throughout the scene I gave the actor that intention to be expressed in physical terms, which kept the scene active and alive and gave the wordplay a

skeleton framework to hang onto for both the actor
and the audience.

The first scene introduces a comic device used
throughout the play, first by the King and later by
Rosaline, Boyet, the Princess, Nathaniel, and Armado—
the letter. The letters are always instruments of humor
rather than exposition. At first I did not know what to
do with them, or what effect they would have on an
audience. But it soon became apparent that if I got the
actor to make his internal reactions external, to continually show us his reaction to the letter—puzzlement,
delight, laughter, dismay—it kept the content very
alive. It is as if a scene is being played between the
sender and the receiver. In place of having Don Armado
and Navarre actually appear together in a scene, we are
given the illusion that they do by having Navarre relate
to the letter as he would relate to Don Armado. Only
now as I am writing do I realize that this was surely
Shakespeare's intent—to keep these characters apart until the very end of the play, for a variety of reasons.
Structurally, it is interesting to separate Don Armado
from the high-born characters. The social makeup of
the Court society is mirrored in the comic scenes with
Don Armado, who seems a free adaptation of Navarre
himself, laying down edicts and modes of behavior. The
letter device also avoids what certainly would be an
unsympathetic portrait of Navarre if Shakespeare created a confrontation between Navarre and Armado, and
we saw the King literally treat Armado in the patronizing and cruel manner suggested by ". . . I love to hear
him lie,/ And I will use him for my minstrelsy" (172–
173).

Don Armado's letter to Navarre heightens our expectation of meeting him, which we do in scene two.
The letter sets him up beautifully as a pompous man

and a phony scholar in love with himself, a verbose, superficial character, interested more in form than in content.

Does it seem shocking to find Navarre as part of a routine—a comic routine, at that—with Costard? He becomes a straight man for Costard. This is only acceptable if you have already created a very human character. If he is presented, as I have often seen him, as stiff and priggish, it would be impossible for him to take part in this routine. He is too knowing to be innocent, and to be unaware of the wordplay makes him a victim of Costard and a rather dull person—good reason for an audience to ignore him. If Navarre is someone who can understand a Costard and in good humor join with him in making this fun, he becomes humanized. *Love's Labor's Lost* is often mislabeled "brittle" and "inconsequential" for lack of finding those qualities to which I keep referring, those warm, real, human qualities, that all the characters truly possess.

It is interesting that Shakespeare has the King, Longaville, and Dumaine exit, leaving Berowne with Costard. It immediately links these two wits together, and somehow you do feel that they are the heroes of the play—perhaps one is the hero and the other the antihero. They both end up in a pickle at the end, "hoist with [their] own petard," as it were. They are both good-natured knaves of a sort, because in truth Berowne is as much a knave as Costard. Berowne talks people into and out of ideas as surely as Costard talks his way into and out of trouble.

ACT I, SCENE II.
"Enter Armado, [a Braggart,] and Moth, his Page."

After reading through the second scene a number of times and trying to understand the humor, much of which escaped me at first, my initial reaction was that it is all talk, talk, talk. What is happening? What are they *doing*? These are the first questions I ask. Armado is instructing Moth, and Moth is instructing Armado, but it is not a "teaching" scene, although there is an element of teacher-pupil in it. What is the underlying nature of the relationship of master-servant, teacher-pupil? Above all, there seems to be affection here that ties the two of them together. I wanted to find an activity for the scene that would help define, or illustrate, if you will, that love between them—and, even further, a dependence between them. Why does Shakespeare introduce Armado with *Moth* except to bring our attention to this relationship? He might just as well have brought Armado in with Costard or Jaquenetta, or Nathaniel and Holofernes.

Then I go back a step and ask myself, "What is a character like Don Armado doing in this Court of Navarre? How did he get there?" And my fantasy suggests that Armado is someone of education, perhaps even of some birthright. He has attached himself to the Court of Navarre as a means of livelihood. True or not, the important thing is that Don Armado *thinks* of himself as someone with a birthright, and in his fantasy he conceives of himself as an educated man. All together, he evokes a personage of shreds and patches: a roving troubadour, of the spirit rather than of song; a Don Quixote who has an exaggerated, unrealistic mystique about chivalry, knighthood, highborn people, proprieties, and moralities, while continually being victimized by the baser side of his nature. I tried then to find a way of dramatizing this in the activity, or "life," of the scene.

Armado is obviously not really a man of refinement: He is one who *aspires* to refinement, aspires to real knowledge, as he aspires to appearance. Appearance means a great deal to him but he does not have the wherewithal. An image began to appear of somebody who tries to "keep up appearances." His clothes are remnants of more glorious days, but falling apart and in need of repair. I therefore conceived first of a costume that was made up of clothes that either were cast off by someone of wealth or had once been his own fine garments that now had to be basted, repaired, and patched. The costume included rusted pieces of fine armor and a rakish feather in his hat, which was a little besotted and broken, so that no matter how Don Armado strutted, the fall of his feather belied the puffiness of his chest.

My questions and presuppositions began to lead me to the "activity" of the scene. Don Armado entered, covered with a cloak and followed by Moth, both of them looking offstage surreptitiously. They appeared suspicious and strange, which gave them a "fantastic" entrance. What were they looking for? What were they concerned about? Their initial impact was slightly comic, which I reinforced with a comic music cue. When Armado seemed satisfied that they were alone, he threw open his cloak and revealed the unadorned man, dressed in his hair shirt, a garment somewhat resembling woolen underwear. I wanted the audience to see Don Armado for what he really is, and then to see how he covers himself up. Thus the "life" of the scene is fulfilled by Moth dressing and actually sewing Armado together. The action reflected his personality— one of covering up, of sewing himself together, of patching himself up, with the affectionate help of Moth, who aids and abets him. They are partners to a deception and are mutually dependent.

Armado talks about sadness and melancholy and his

love. The theme of sweet sadness is characteristic of Armado throughout the play. As I said before, he borders on a character that we pity, even as we laugh at him. However, I wanted the audience to feel tenderly toward him and not to accept him as simply the grotesque butt of everyone's jokes. He deserves better. None of his actions or intrigues are destructive, as are those planned by Malvolio in *Twelfth Night*, for instance. Armado's letter-writing and his intriguing are of a gentle, slightly befuddled, college-professor type. We see a somewhat tired, worldly man pitted against the *brio* of youth—the hope that springs eternal, the inexhaustive energy of inventiveness and ideas we attribute to innocence.

For the second part of the scene I wanted to find an action that would show us the competition between Armado and Costard for Jaquenetta, and would show that Armado is really no threat to Costard, except in his own mind. I also wished to show the inventiveness of Costard and Jaquenetta in dealing with the situation, for both rustics are, in their natural, shrewd, commonsense way, more than a match for the more "brilliant," knowing, and sophisticated Armado. I staged the scene as a sort of continuous dance—Armado was paying court to Jaquenetta, while she was reassuring Costard, who was throwing kisses and affirmations of love from behind Armado's back to Jaquenetta, who was finally pulled off by Dull.

The remainder of the scene is a contest between Armado and Costard: Costard is trying to get away, and Armado, the vested authority, is trying to restrain him in every way. The scene ends with Armado's marvelous and ridiculous soliloquy, which is so outrageous, and his excess of verbiage, emotion, and analysis of the situation so foolish, that the only way to make him anything more than an absolute fool is to make him a believable and honest creation, subject to inexplicable but lovable excesses.

ACT II, SCENE I.
"Enter the Princess of France, with three attending Ladies, [Rosaline, Maria, Katharine,] and three Lords, [one of whom is Boyet]."

As director I ask myself: "Where did they come from? What are they doing? What can I do to make them and their relationships clear for an audience, supportive to what the words tell me?" I have to give them an entrance that marks the beginning of a new section, so it must be of a certain importance. I have to show that the Princess is someone of royal stature, with attending ladies. Her coming for a state visit would suggest that she brought a lot of trappings with her—clothes, presents, anything else to make her comfortable in a strange court and impress them with her wealth and power. (You might ask, "How does the Queen of England travel to Canada for a state visit?") Later in this scene it is indicated that the girls have previously met Longaville, Dumaine, and Berowne. They have looked forward to this visit, and they arrive with some expectation and excitement. It is rather like Smith girls going to Harvard for a weekend visit. This high expectation, enthusiasm, delight, and gaiety about everything the ladies do, makes me think they have not traveled very much. They are bubbly and girlish under a veneer of sophistication. Boyet is their duenna, confidant, and chaperone. He is like a mother hen, instructing them and running after them.

A post horn is heard from offstage signaling their arrival. Squads of servants issue forth to carry their luggage and there is a constant crisscross of upstage activity during the arrival scene. The ladies—Katharine, Maria, and Rosaline—arrive, preceding the Princess. They are young, eager, excited girls who cannot repress their ebullience and run on ahead of the Princess.

Then the Princess enters. She is followed by a page carrying a huge umbrella to shade her from the sun. The girls pull her toward the fountain; they invite her to look at the telescope; they show her the loveliness of the towers, the garden around. One senses the very warm and strong interrelationship of these girls as human beings, not just as handmaidens to a queen. The Princess herself is caught up in the enthusiasm and delight of Rosaline, Maria, and Katharine, so that Boyet is obliged to sober her up: "Now, madam, summon up your dearest spirits" (1).

The ladies often use Boyet as the butt of their jokes, to which he willingly acquiesces. A warm and intimate relationship between Boyet and the ladies is necessary; otherwise Boyet is in danger of becoming a high class messenger, hardly meriting Berowne's attention in Act Five. Boyet was placed as a man of dedicated service, whatever form that service might take—whether it be as the Princess' fool or the true and devoted servant of his master.

Let us consider the Princess. What a delightful character! She is so intelligent; she has such a wonderful sense of humor! She had never seemed so to me in other productions. Rosaline seemed to be the only sparkplug and always seemed to take over the show, as it were. From the text, however, it becomes apparent that the Princess initiates most of the fun and most of the activity. If she is allowed to be a warm human being from the very beginning all of that seems in good taste. If she is played coldly or primly, or the dignified aspects of being a princess are overemphasized, then her later

initiative in some of the foolish and silly love games
seems inappropriate.

Her first speech to Boyet (13) seems very formal
and "put on." Examined closely, it seems to parallel
Boyet's manner, as if the Princess were meeting him on
his own ground. Later she seems to mingle informally
with the girls equally as well. After reading through the
play once, one might wonder: "Well, what kind of a
character is this who can be both silly and dignified?"
I came to the conclusion that Eleanor is a human being
rather than a conventionalized princess who, when in
love, can be very foolish, very silly, even giddy, and yet
has been schooled in graces and a sense of duty. She
has been entrusted with a diplomatic mission. Boyet
was not sent alone. Why not? Perhaps because the wise
old King thought his daughter a much more persuasive
weapon of diplomacy in this affair. As it turned out, he
was quite right.

The Princess sends Boyet off to report on Narvarre's
intentions. With Boyet gone and a little time on their
hands, the girls exchange confidences, gossip, and small
talk. They talk about their boyfriends, Berowne, Longaville, and Dumaine. They are powdering their noses and
arranging their curls. Their language seems formal. But
is this not merely "form"? Even so, it must not hide
the real nature of the moment. What seems to be mere
exposition and the staking out of each girl's claim for
her man becomes something more, I think, in Shakespeare's hands. It becomes a familiar, affectionate action
—the exchange of confidences. It is obvious by their
choice of words that the girls are passionately in love
with these men. Their descriptions are fantastically excessive in praise—even the rather sharp and impenetra-
ble Rosaline seems to have her defenses down here. The
Princess says, "God bless my ladies! Are they all in

love,/ That every one her own hath garnishèd/ With
such bedecking ornaments of praise?" (77–79). There
is a gentle criticism in the words "garnishèd" and
"bedecking ornaments"—also, perhaps, a touch of envy,
since the Princess has no love. Has not Shakespeare
introduced this note of wistfulness to heighten the impact when the Princess falls in love, at first sight, with
Navarre?

The playscript then says, "Enter Navarre, Longaville,
Dumaine, and Berowne" (88). The King enters with
a small flourish and the Princess and the King bow to
each other and then open up a formal discussion. But
what is the acting subtext *beneath* the words? Note that
immediately the Princess attacks Navarre in a light,
sharp, and humorous way. It could be played in an
imperious manner as if she were demanding her way
("I will be welcome, then. Conduct me thither." [95]),
but how unpleasant, how against the nature of this
sunny comedy. The Princess certainly has the best of
the encounter, which suggests that either the King is
not as clever as she, or he is caught off guard. Could
it be that he is surprised and delighted by the Princess'
looks and manner? How consistent of Shakespeare to
give this formal moment a humorous twist. He does
not sacrifice their dignity, but he does not forget that
they are human beings.

The Princess is firm but gracious, and shows both
independence and tact. The lines indicate that she gives
him a document to read, and the King and the Princess
suddenly stop talking. Berowne and Rosaline begin to
talk, in what would seem to be a private conversation.
They banter back and forth as if searching out each
other, challenging one another. Berowne throws down
a gauntlet and Rosaline throws it right back at him.
Again, the lady seems to have the best of the encounter.

Rosaline retains her humor and her sharpness, while
Berowne loses his composure. At this point I wonder,
"But what is happening to the King and the Princess?"
I have to assume that they have been concerned with
the paper. However, after Navarre leaves, Boyet says,
"Navarre is infected" (228), and proceeds to describe
Navarre's conduct in this scene. Something has to happen while Navarre and the Princess read the document
to set the audience up for what is later made manifest
to them in words: Navarre has fallen in love with the
Princess. The Princess of France and Navarre resume
their conversation, a discussion of the business details
of the document, how much was owed whom and how
much land—it is simply a land transaction. As the
director, one tends to look askance and say, "Well, what
is that doing in here, what relevance does it have to
this light, charming comedy of love—it really is boring
and filled with a lot of words we don't understand,
people we don't see, past events, and it doesn't move
the action forward, so couldn't we just cut a lot of it?"
But when I question why it is there, I realize that what
is probably happening during this conversation is that
the two of them are losing their place, falling in love
while trying to pull themselves back to the mundane
document itself.

Shakespeare gives us only one actual love encounter
in this section—Berowne and Rosaline—which has to
stand for the rest. True to the characters and to Shakespeare's own wonderful invention and sense of fun, it
is not a conversation of love, it is a sparring match—
Round One, as it were. The overconfident Berowne
sidles up to Rosaline with the utmost assurance and
uses one of the oldest lines in history. The line sounds
so completely contemporary that its presence in this
play makes one realize it is absolutely ancient. "Did not

I dance with you in Brabant once?" (113)—as if to
say, "Didn't I see you at the homecoming dance?"
or "Didn't I see you at the goat ritual last Dionysia?"
or something. Then Rosaline, very neatly, instead of
falling flat on her face in raptures, proceeds to put him
in his place.

Throughout the play the girls seem far superior to
the men. They handle the men with great assurance and
aplomb, and with great humor. The male ego is de-
flated—this is always an amusing subject for comedy
and one of Shakespeare's favorites, but his genius turns
it to more than comic use. At the moment when the
whole mood of the play turns upon the death of
the King of France, the girls suddenly realize that the
"game" is over and that they have spent an inordinate
amount of time playing a game, instead of comporting
themselves directly and speaking straight to the point.
Although there is fun in winning the game, how is
success measured if the match is lost?

Our attention is drawn from the Berowne-Rosaline
match to the faltering discussion of the King and the
Princess, and when the Princess asks Boyet to produce
further proof of her claim (159), Boyet says, "So please
your Grace, the packet is not come/ Where that and
other specialties are bound./ To-morrow you shall have
a sight of them" (162–164). One wonders, when the
Princess turns with such confidence to Boyet and when
Boyet proves to have been such a capable minister and
always so throughly in command, how he would indeed
fail to bring these important papers with him. I thought
that perhaps Boyet was taking advantage of the moment to extend the encounter between the ladies and
the young men, knowing, as a good diplomat, that the
ladies' beauty and charm might very well win his point
even more strongly than documents.

After accompanying the King offstage, Dumaine and Longaville sneak back to corner Boyet and find out more about their ladies (192). The ladies collected around the fountain, center stage, and while seeming to be exchanging gossip and small talk behind their fans, were really keeping an eye peeled toward Boyet and the furtive questioning of Dumaine and Longaville. The coupling of Longaville and Maria, Katharine and Dumaine was pointed up by having the girls seem particularly interested when their corresponding partner was questioning Boyet.

The language when the girls resume talking is very bawdy (213). If one has ever listened in on the private hen sessions of the most literate and chaste young school girls, one is not at all shocked to hear Katharine and Maria carry on in this lusty way. Throughout the play, the girls are clever and knowing in their references to sex and love. Originally these girls were played by boys, and it is quite possible they got away with even more than is indicated here. But I must say that in our production this bawdy talk in no way affected the charm of the girls. It rather made them more interesting, lively, and sophisticated to be joking in this manner. Surely the key to this scene is not in the bawdiness or the lines, but in the fun, the fun of released feelings, of "putting on" Boyet.

During all this the Princess is notably silent. One wonders what is going on in her mind, until Boyet singles her out and says, "Navarre is infected" (228). And she rather innocently says, "With what?" as if she were really puzzled. Boyet says, "With that which we lovers entitle affected" (230). And then he goes on to present a most lovely song of love and indicate that, to his clear mind and eye, the King has fallen in love with her. The Princess does not answer. She says, "Come to our pavilion. Boyet is disposed" (248). It is an evasion. Her sudden departure is necessitated by the need to cover up, for she has fallen in love with Navarre.

ACT III, SCENE I.
"Enter [Armado, the] Braggart, and [Moth,] his Boy."

The humor in this scene seems to be the most obscure and difficult in the play. Much of it is madcap humor for its own sake. It is just fun—word fun, nonsense, like that found in a Marx Brothers' routine. This, as the other comic scenes in the play, worked brilliantly in performance. The second section begins, "Enter [Moth, the] Page, and [Costard, the] Clown," and starts with the lines, "A wonder, master! Here's a costard broken in a shin" (63). Armado mistakes the intent, or pretends to, and they are off, into the business about "l'envoy," and "egma," "riddle," and "The fox, the ape," etc. Neither I nor the actors knew what to do with this, and although the footnotes very carefully explain the meaning of every word and expression, they do not answer the questions "What is it about?" and "What makes it work in the theater?" The first reaction, of course, is to cut it. That is the easiest of all solutions when dealing with obscurity in a Shakespearean play. Even if one understands the allusions after careful study, one wonders if a modern audience will. But I have almost always found that the humor does not lie in the words. I would like to emphasize that point very strongly. The essence of an *emotion* in Shakespeare, in poetry, is almost always in the words. But it certainly is not the solution to *comedy*. In my work in Shakespeare comedy—*A Midsummer Night's Dream, The Taming of the Shrew, The Comedy of Errors, The Tempest, As You Like It,* and *Love's Labor's Lost*—

I have learned to trust Shakespeare's theatrical sense. I recognize the classic base of his humor, the ageless theatrical forms and kinds of comedy that are still evident in contemporary theater, including night clubs, burlesque, television, and the Broadway theater. Abbott and Costello, Martin and Lewis, Bobby Clark, Bert Lahr, and Red Skelton have all used the same routines as Shakespeare's clowns.

I recognized this section of Act III (65 ff.) as a comic routine, a nonsense routine. To try to make sense out of the literary allusions or mistakes in hearing as the footnotes suggest (that "salve" is a mispronunciation of "salvé," or "plantain" refers to broken shins), gets one nowhere on the stage. I asked myself, "What is the nature of this routine?" There are three people on stage—Armado, Moth, and Costard—which does seem to fit the first lyric ("The fox, the ape, and the humble-bee/ Were still at odds, being but three." [77–78]). Now that is not a difficult allusion to understand. I mean the number "three" is odd. We could refer to Armado as the fox, Costard as the ape, and Moth as the humble-bee. I think it makes no difference who might be what, but the ape seems to fit Armado's and Moth's feelings about Costard, and the humble-bee, the busy, busy bee, seems to fit Moth well, which leaves the fox for Armado. I then took the term "goose" (83) literally, and the three characters worked out a rather charming routine that included the "goosing" of one or another of them. The routine finishes with, "A good l'envoy, ending in the goose" (91), which seems to make very clear the author's intent of what this routine must have been— vulgar and bawdy! The question then becomes one of taste—of suggestion rather than explicitness, titillation rather than horselaughs, a certain grace or charm in its execution rather than vulgarity—to have it conform to the texture of the whole play. The audience recognized it as a routine; they enjoyed the "who's on first" analogue of it, and enjoyed its bawdiness.

Underlying the whole "routine" section is Costard's constant intention for as long as he remains a prisoner —escape. Costard starts the routine as a way to divert Armado's intention—overseeing his prisoner. He so confuses Armado with his double-talking that Armado has to cut off the conversation in order to clear his brain. By the time we come to the line, "O, marry me to one Frances! I smell some l'envoy, some goose, in this" (113–114), Costard has entered very much into the spirit of this semi-burlesque double-talking kind of confusion. In our production, the scene had reached such a pitch that almost every line following this was a laugh line. Not that the audience understood the literal word *sense* of it, but they were participating in the word *fun* of it. A rhythm of laughter had started, and it reached a pitch and height of hilarity which can be maintained, provided the ball is kept in the air. If a director learns to recognize similar obscure passages in Shakespeare as comic routines, he will find, more often than not, that they work with this approach to the playing. Many of the scenes in *Love's Labor's Lost* that did not appear at all funny in print were very funny on stage in our production, and related to the same kind of humor we still laugh at today.

Following Armado and Moth's exit (126), Berowne enters surreptitiously, sneaking on, which reflects the way Armado was first seen and the way Longaville and Dumaine encountered Boyet. Everyone is beginning to have secrets from everyone else. In this scene, I feel we have the high-class con man meeting the low-class con man, and Berowne is forced to see himself for what he is—another version of Costard. He must employ

Costard to do the dirty work that he should be doing
himself.

What a wonderful soliloquy of Berowne follows, one
of self-discovery, in which he struggles with what he
knows to be the truth of himself. This soliloquy saves
the character from being pompous and egotistical,
or self-satisfied and morally superior to the others—
all rather unpleasant characteristics. By showing us
Berowne's struggle and subsequent defeat by Cupid,
Shakespeare allows us to admire Berowne. This soliloquy is explicit in its investigation of how useless the
defenses of logic and habit are against the illogic of
passion, which is key to the way Shakespeare develops
his theme in almost every other scene.

ACT IV, SCENE I.
"Enter the Princess, a Forester, her Ladies [Maria,
Katharine, Rosaline], and her Lords [Boyet and
others]."

There are hunting calls to introduce the Princess and
her companions, creating the impression of a large
hunting party and a princely outing with servants. The
ladies are in outdoor hunting outfits, carrying bows
and quivers, and enter at a run to give the sense of the
chase in starting off the scene. The party pauses to rest,
and the Princess says, with some regret, "Well, lords,
to-day we shall have our dispatch;/ On Saturday we will
return to France" (5–6). It is the day after their
arrival and they are to leave the next day, so all in all
they will have been in Navarre for only three days.

Then follows the exchange between the Princess and
the Forester about hunting (7 ff.), which seems to have
very little relevance to the play, aside from the obvious
point that it is a section with grace of language and
shows the Princess to be a woman of humor, wit, and

sensitivity. It certainly does not further the plot. However, it does introduce, for a very brief moment, the element that is to return at the end of the play with the news of the death of the King of France. For a moment, the Princess reflects rather pensively on death and dying and on the more serious feelings that flow beneath life's fun, games, and giddiness (24). This section is essential to the play, for what it does to round out the character of the Princess and, primarily, for its foreshadowing of the somber tone at the play's end.

As Shakespeare repeatedly and so artfully accomplishes, this exchange succeeds in setting up a contrasting mood for the sudden entrance of Costard. The Princess immediately comes out of her melancholy and begins to banter with Costard. Costard has accidentally mixed up the letters, so the letter Berowne intended for Rosaline gets misplaced and the letter Armado wrote to Jaquenetta is delivered to Rosaline by mistake. My previous remarks about letters apply here to the letter Boyet reads. In order to preserve the fun and the jest, the lines, "This letter is mistook; it importeth none here./ It is writ to Jaquenetta" (58–59), are said in confidence to the Princess, so that as Boyet reads it aloud, Rosaline still thinks it was meant for her. Her reaction is one of pride, parading the fact that she is the only one who has received a letter. This changes to a growing dismay as the letter is read. It exhibits such bad form and clumsiness of language that Rosaline can not conceive of Berowne's writing such a poor letter. Finally, I directed her to snatch it away from Boyet and read the last lines herself: "Thus, expecting thy reply, I profane my lips on thy foot, my eyes on thy picture, and my heart on thy every part" (82–84). Only when she reads the signature, "Don Adriano de Armado," does she realize that the joke has been on her and that Berowne has not written the letter at all. She evidences a sense of relief that releases itself in playful anger at Boyet for making her the butt of the joke. Boyet takes the letter back and Rosaline continues fuming at him in mock anger. Boyet makes the lines, "Thus dost thou hear the Nemean lion roar/ 'Gainst thee, thou lamb, that standest as his prey" (87–88), refer to Rosaline's reaction to his prank.

When the Princess leaves, she says, "Here, sweet, put up this; 'twill be thine another day" (106). She is referring back to Rosaline and her somewhat hang-dog expression after having her expectations aroused and then dashed. As the Princess and attendants skim offstage to continue the hunt, Boyet and Rosaline lag behind. Rosaline is a little peeved and annoyed at Boyet, in a playful way, and Boyet continues to tease her. They each take the measure of the other, and Rosaline draws her bow at him mock-threateningly, as she snaps back, "Why, she that bears the bow" (108). Each tries to top the other and have the last word in a lusty, bawdy series of references. The audience seemed to understand and enjoy the exchange, not because of the bawdy references but because of the teasing. It was played with charm, grace, and an air of sophistication. The audience was also tuned in to the reaction of Costard, who very well understands what is going on and almost outdoes them in the bawdy by-play. In Costard's attitude there is a suggestion of, "Oh my, oh my, how the high-born do go on! The high-born do almost go on like the low-born."

ACT IV, SCENE II.
"Enter Dull, Holofernes the Pedant, and Nathaniel."

I began this scene with suggestions of the hunt still going on, Holofernes and Nathaniel barreling on and calling, "Sola, Sola," as if it were a hunting cry, and Dull entering with grumpy indignation, a misaimed arrow through his hat. This ties the entrance of Holofernes and Nathaniel to those in the preceding scene. Nathaniel's line, "Very reverend sport, truly, and done in the testimony of a good conscience" (1–2), refers directly to what has just gone on. It is as if they had been caught in the direct path of the chase.

What do you do with Holofernes and Nathaniel in a contemporary production, since all the usual footnotes refer to their humor and character types in relation to an Elizabethan audience? One needn't ask. They work beautifully for the modern audience; they are classic types, Holofernes being the dogmatic, narrow-minded, superior tyrant of the pedantic intellect, and Nathaniel representing the hostile sycophant that one often finds close at the heels of a Holofernes. They are birds of a feather, and yet fall into a king-subject enslavement. In order to physically dramatize this, I had Nathaniel, at the opening of the scene, slightly behind Holofernes, as if he would never walk abreast but always slightly behind his Master.

Their hostile camaraderie begins when Nathaniel, under the guise of admiring Holofernes, attacks him. He uses words like "the epithets are sweetly varied, like a scholar" (8–9) and then proceeds to argue with Holofernes. (On the other hand, when Dull attacks Holofernes, Nathaniel jumps to his defense.)

At first the actors did not know what to do with the material. The words confused them; the Latin expressions seemed to disturb them. They would say, "I can't pronounce them well," or "What do they mean?" However, I think this is *exactly* the humor that Shakespeare intended—the *characters* do not know what the words mean. And Nathaniel and Holofernes do not know how to pronounce Latin correctly. Thus the actor finds himself in the identical predicament of the character.

In order to conceal his ignorance, Nathaniel has a little book in which he constantly looks up definitions of some of Holofernes' wilder expressions or else writes them down for future reference. Holofernes is always the teacher. He teaches everyone (and so I had him carry a blackboard pointer). He is never at a loss for words because he makes up words. He makes them sound both important and Latin. This pose is as meaningful to an audience today as it must have been to an Elizabethan audience. I can only judge this by the fact that, without adding any sight gags, the material produced gales of laughter in the audience. It seems not to matter, for instance, that the audience understand what "pomewater" is, or "the ear of coelo" (4–5), or that Holofernes does not make sense. They understand that his words are hollow (Holofernes = Hollow Furnace = hot air).

A great deal of this comedy one cannot get with the eye, from the printed page. It is comedy for the ear. The sound of the words make for great humor; the joke is in the sound rather than the sense. I am sure that "pricket" (12), "facere" (14), and "bis coctus" (21) made their own fun in Shakespeare's time simply by their sound. They make the same fun today. Those who maintain that the humor in *Love's Labor's Lost* is impossible for a contemporary audience to enjoy, or try to make sense of footnotes, would save themselves both time and anguish by simply performing it in front of an audience. Trust the material. If you let it work for itself, it will.

Nathaniel and Holofernes are rich in character and are much more than superficial comic prototypes. Their material need not be reduced to a stand-up comic level.

It depends on the use, the sense, and, in this case, the corruption of language for its humor. To me, this humor must have been an inside joke to Shakespeare, for he, who so brilliantly handles verbiage and verbal characters, has created two sets of comics in this play who massacre the language—Armado, who massacres the form and indulges in overelaborate imagery, and Holofernes and Nathaniel, who shred the language apart, utterly destroying it.

ACT IV, SCENE III.
"Enter Berowne with a paper in his hand, alone."

I used Act IV, scene iii to mark the end of the first act of our production. It rises to a wonderful pitch of dynamics, and it has a great deal of humor. The threads of plot and intention entwine as the boys go off to create a divertissement and make a frontal attack on the enemy camp.

I am not at all sure that this scene can be fully appreciated in print. In the theater, it is very rich and magnificently funny, and the humor seems to multiply in greater proportion to each element added. It is absolutely essential that the audience see the reactions of Berowne, the King, Longaville, and Dumaine, as each of these suitors enters in turn to read his love poem while the previous one hides. At first Berowne is the only one whose "betrayal" is undiscovered; the other three do not suspect he has also broken his ascetic vow. It temporarily places him in a position of superior moral posturing, and I gave him an Olympian height, the cupola above, from which to play—a heaven from which to observe these lowly groundlings beneath him—and also a height from which to tumble from grace. Berowne plays with the total inner joy that comes with a position of superiority. He plays hurt and righteous, the

indignant preserver of tradition, oath, and propriety, to
the hilt. As Costard approaches with the letter exposing
Berowne (183), the anticipation of events to come
seems to quadruple the audience's enjoyment. There is
suddenly a great leap of humor that has been carefully
prepared for, the moment when Berowne, on the brink
of triumph, is reduced to the charming sophist fake
that he is.

Note how different each of the men's poems are and
how rich they are in character. To me, the King's verse
is very lovely and loving; if it has a fault, it is too
romantic. But it does not seem ridiculous when one
hears it. The problem thus arises of showing the shallowness of the passion in order to keep the tone of
the play at a certain level of involvement. It is not,
or should not be, deep passion. The King never had
more than a cursory look at the Princess during their
one public encounter, so his love comes from intuition
and a first-sight view, rather than from thoughtful
understanding. I thought it necessary to dramatize the
superficiality underlying his expression of passion, so
when the King talked about "tears of mine" (28), he
reached into the fountain and delicately splashed his
face with water to suggest the tears he would like to
have felt.

Longaville's poem is a great deal less graceful than
the King's—more simple-minded and stiff, rather formal
and exact. This led me to define Longaville's character
as rather precise and pedantic. (Mind you, all that I say
about the character of these young men is superseded
by their high good spirits and joyous participation in
life and living.)

Because the actor was a slender fellow and his character's name was Longaville, I gave him a long, thin
scroll for his poem. The poem was hidden inside his

book, much as a student might hide a comic book within his textbook for fear of discovery. As Longaville is walking and reading, this long scroll suddenly rolls down from his book and he realizes he has been exposed. He looks around and, seeing no one, throws all caution to the winds and begins to proclaim his passion. Dumaine announces his presence with a great groan offstage; Longaville looks for some place to hide and, seeing none, throws his poem into the fountain and runs downstage to hide as best he can on the fore-steps of the stage.

Dumaine is the least reserved of the group and, perhaps, a little less bright than the others. Looking back on their original oaths, one recalls that Longaville talked about the mind as his jumping-off place, whereas Dumaine talked about sensual things. At the height of Dumaine's passion, Longaville tips off the audience with a wink that he is going to move in on the situation, and then he calls, "Dumaine," who at first can not place where the voice is coming from. Longaville reveals himself and Dumaine reacts with panic, shame, and fear, in that order. Then the King steps out, and as he laces into Dumaine and Longaville, we see Berowne warming up for the final kill, and we anticipate his attack. As the King smugly ties up his arguments and begins to march off in high dudgeon, Dumaine and Longaville are in attitudes of terrible chagrin and immeasurable remorse.

Berowne reveals himself at this point and mirthfully but mercilessly exploits the situation. He flagellates them with words, treats them condescendingly, pats them patronizingly on the head—including the King. He evokes images of the naughty child, the wilful lawbreaker, the corrupter of social order. He assumes the role of King, lawgiver, justice-deliverer, prison warden, teacher, mother, father, and any and all personages of authority, and the others have to sit and take it. At that moment we are all wondering what is going to happen to Berowne. He is in the catbird seat and doing quite well, but how long will he remain seated? Finally, Longaville, Dumaine, and the King unite in self-defense and desperation, as Berowne goes on and on and on. They fear that his extemporaneous wit will never cease and they will be subject to it for the rest of their days. The King, their spokesman, says, "Too bitter is thy jest./ Are we betrayed thus to thy over-view?" (169–170), a reference which was one of the factors that led me to use towers on the set.

But in truth, Shakespeare allows Berowne to go on in this way to give him enough rope for Costard's noose. Berowne is finally unmasked and undone by the innocent Jaquenetta and her letter; he has been unmasked by a fool. Now the four men are all of a kind, and misery loves company.

How wonderfully Shakespeare twists and turns the theme of unmasking! With the exception of this scene, it is the woman who invariably unmasks the man. This happens to all the major male characters—the four young nobles (with their Russian disguises, V. ii.), Don Armado and Costard (V. ii.), and even Holofernes (IV. ii.). No matter what a man appears to be, or what posture he assumes, he is subverted by love, passion, and sex, variously, almost in direct proportion to his degree of intellectual refinement and pretension.

Being unmasked, the King brings them back to their senses by suddenly realizing, "Are we not *all* in love?" (277). And with that, they all moan and groan, lost in their private passion and pain, remembering their loves. Their true, loving, healthy, masculine natures are revealed and accepted by themselves. They now see their

initial act of forswearing love and feminine company as
unnatural. They look to Berowne for help. "O some
authority how to proceed;/ Some tricks, some quillets,
how to cheat the devil" (282–283). They want to salve
their consciences somehow, and of course, they have
chosen the right man—Berowne can easily make black
seem white and white seem black. He proceeds to do
so with his own magnificent illogic, proving that love is
the road to knowledge and that within the eyes of a
woman one finds the spur to all learning (345 ff.). This
passage, in its utter surrender to emotion and pure
joy, obliterates that unnatural order imposed in the
beginning.

Without being made to look ridiculous, they become
childlike and effervescent, buoyant with boyish spirits.
Yet, by establishing the play firmly on "real" behavior,
one knows that these men are now capable of love, not
merely posturing. They march off with new vigor, but
still planning to mask themselves, à la Russe. Soon,
however, Shakespeare intends to strip them of even this
shallow device to make them face the young ladies as
they are.

ACT V, SCENE I.
"Enter [Holofernes,] the Pedant, [Nathaniel,] the
Curate, and Dull, [the Constable]."

The second act of our production began with Act V,
scene i, which resembles the controlled madness of the
Mad Tea Party. (When I refer to our first act in this
discussion, I am referring to all scenes up to Act V,
scene i, of this edition. The exploration of the situation
is dealt with through Act IV, scene iii. Act V deals
with bringing the problems to their resolution and is
sufficiently rich in content to bear the weight of an
act division. This also allowed me to start the second

act with a comic scene, which served to whet the audience for the final confrontation.) Holofernes, Nathaniel, and Dull enter, just finishing up from dinner. Dull enters chewing on a chicken leg and washing it down with some wine from a flask; Holofernes and Nathaniel, bellies lined with capon and exuding satisfaction, are casually strolling and exchanging bon mots and what passes for erudition.

The sound of the language suffices in itself for humor, if said with great panache and in a matter-of-fact manner. Every word is pronounced as written, but without any finesse or educated accent, Holofernes and Nathaniel spewing out this "language" and anything else that comes to their minds with great flair and self-assurance.

Holofernes' attitude toward Don Armado in this scene is a competitive one (9 ff.). He is picky and critical of him. I inferred from this that he was jealous of Armado's taking upon himself the mantle of erudition for this group. Armado sets himself up as the arbiter of custom and language, and feels free to educate and inform both those above and below him in station. This is direct competition for Holofernes, who, thrashing around with his wicked tongue and malformed brain, whacks out at Armado. He also manages to get in a few digs at Nathaniel, treating him like a naughty student.

Moth and Costard act as a kind of antiphonal chorus in this scene (35 ff.), relating in turn to each other and the mad trio and to the audience, *i.e.*, setting up their own jokes, trapping Holofernes, Nathaniel, and Armado, and then delivering the coup de grâce to the audience. Holofernes is driven mad with exasperation by Moth; Armado acts delighted but patronizing toward Moth's wit.

At the suggestion of putting on some antic, Holofernes leaps with joy and proceeds with the kind of childish delight that is characteristic of all amateur theatrics—plus all the elements of jealousy, ego, and temperament—as to who should get the biggest part and who the smallest part. The mismatched egotists exit excitedly, united for the moment at the prospect of presenting their "antic" (a most appropriate choice of word).

ACT V, SCENE II.
"Enter the Ladies [Princess, Katharine, Rosaline, and Maria]."

Rather than have the ladies appear at the same time, I had them enter one by one, so that I could see their individual reactions to their poems and accompanying favors. The staging of the scene paralleled the beginning of Act IV, scene iii. First the Princess enters at the top of the tower with a poem and a bracelet of diamonds. From there she can see the other three enter. Maria arrives with a long poem and a long string of pearls from Longaville. Then Katharine appears with Dumaine's poem and a glove; and finally, Rosaline enters with her poem and a pendant from Berowne. The Princess observes them, all oblivious to their surroundings, walking and reading their notes with rapt attention. She cannot suppress her laughter and they realize they have been discovered. They look up from their poems in surprise, and then, chagrin.

The next part of the scene was conceived as a teasing game for the girls. They are like young college girls, no more than seventeen or eighteen, somewhat embarrassed, yet delighted and giddy with the idea of new-found love—particularly the Princess. One gets the feeling that the Princess has been too wrapped up in state affairs, and has been kept too close to home by a sickly father—always tending to her duties and never

permitting herself the luxury of romance. Here with just
her companions, she is at long last letting herself go.
The scene has the feeling of a hen party, in which the
girls begin to tease and goad each other on, making
jokes at each other's expense, with no serious intent.

But there is a gentle, sexual teasing going on throughout the scene, which leads to some word play with a
distinct edge between Rosaline and Katharine about
Katharine's flirtatiousness. This section also echoes the
scene of the young men in Act IV, scene iii (255–276).

"Well bandied both, a set of wit well played" (29)—
the Princess puts an end to the game of tease and tag.
They sit, somewhat exhausted but happy, and begin to
share confidences. They are each proud of their separate
lords, and yet wise enough to see their foolishness. They
are both "in" love and outside, observing the process.

The Princess has made them aware that each apparently private communication from lover to love means
that the men are actually in league with one another.
The girls decide to exploit the joke—to humble the
boys and make them aware that love is not to be taken
so lightly, nor affections bought so easily. And as the
Princess says, "None are so surely caught, when they
are catched,/ As wit turned fool" (69–70). In other
words, love makes fools of all.

They begin to plot as the idea catches hold, and they
have just gone into a conspiratorial attitude when Boyet
enters. He brings the news that he has overheard the
men planning an antic for the ladies, to be presented
in disguise. It is important that we recognize the various lovers specifically as Boyet, overcome by the humor
of it all, retells the plan of their disguise as Russian
Muscovites and their purpose to beguile, to court, and
to dance.

The Princess decides what they will do: the ladies

will also mask themselves, and they will trade favors. In that way, each suitor will only be able to identify his lady by the favor she wears, and thus he will woo the wrong girl. The girls quickly embrace the idea and eagerly exchange their favors. The Princess explains that her intent is only to make the merriment greater, "Upon the next occasion that we meet,/ With visages displayed, to talk and greet" (143–144). Notice again that it is the Princess who does the leading, not Rosaline. Although Rosaline suggests another game to her (". . . shall we dance if they desire us to 't?" [145]), it is the Princess who determines their behavior. As the Princess outlines the plan, a lady-in-waiting brings on the masks, and offstage there is a trumpet announcing the men.

The stage directions say, "Enter Blackamoors with music; [Moth,] the Boy, with a speech, and the rest of the Lords disguised" (158). I assumed this meant that a divertissement took place at this point, something to amuse the ladies. At first I thought of having a very professional entertainment—good dancing of some sort with the men and women as onlookers. My second thought, which was more in keeping with the boys' sense of bravura and braggadocio, was for the men themselves, in Muscovite costumes, to attempt the dance. So, preceded by one professional dancer who leads them on with a mandolin, tambourine, and whip, the men rush on stage. Their dance is accompanied by musicians playing something that sounds like Russian folk music.

The men, safely disguised, shamelessly disport themselves in front of the girls. They legitimately and energetically attempt Russian character dancing. The actors, being no more accomplished that Berowne, Longaville, Dumaine, and Navarre would have been, create quite a divertissement. There is no attempt to

be consciously funny but the effect is hilarious. The
humor comes from the costumes, the blunderous dancing, and the knowledge that these are the lovers in
disguise, shamelessly showing off in front of the girls—
rather collegiate, but endearing.

After the dance and Moth's stumbling introduction,
Berowne dismisses Moth in disgust and Rosaline takes
over, wearing the Princess' favor and displaying it in
such an exaggerated manner that the King cannot possibly mistake the fact that she is wearing his favor
on her arm.

The girls proceed to tease the men and lead them on.
The men try to maintain their disguises, including the
Russian accents. The masks that the girls are using (see
"Director's Preparation and Production Notes," V. ii.
127) allow them to share reactions with each other and
the audience and yet keep a false face to the men. The
men, therefore, think they are impressing the girls and
getting away with their antic, while in truth the girls
are doing everything they can to frustrate the men and
make them appear foolish.

The group begins to break up into couples, to allow
for more intimate tête-à-têtes. The action takes the form
of a rather elaborate minuet: while conversing, the
couples walk in different directions around the stage,
and each moves toward center when it is important that
their conversation be overheard. The King asks the disguised Rosaline if she will chat; she replies, "In private
then" (230), and they converse apart. As the King and
Rosaline move out of the center position, Berowne and
the Princess take their place, and as they drift away,
still conversing, Dumaine and Maria move in. They in
turn make way for Katharine and Longaville. The exchange between Katharine and Longaville is the most
difficult and I found no way of making it clear to a

modern audience, although I think the actors and I understood it well. Therefore, we cut lines 252 through 256.

As they all find their private corners, Boyet sums up their behavior to the audience, and I think foreshadows what is to come: "The tongues of mocking wenches [which is an unattractive image] are as keen/ As is the razor's edge invisible" (257–258). Boyet mildly disapproves of what they are doing. The girls are really wasting precious time that they will later wish had been spent in a more loving manner.

The girls, who have driven the men mad with their derision and their mercurial switches from warm and flirtatious to cold and aloof, break off abruptly. The men, in a rage of frustration, rush off with slightly disheveled habits and equally rumpled egos. The girls jeer after them, "Twenty adieus, my frozen Muscovits./ Are these the breed of wits so wondered at?" (266–267). When the men are gone, the girls have a moment of self-delight and smugness. They compare notes on the behavior of their young men and make fun of them quite thoroughly.

The girls re-exchange favors, this time the favor going to the appropriate girl. Rosaline suggests that they compound their ridicule by innocently relating a story to the men about the foolish Muscovites that were shortly there. The aggressiveness with which the girls pursue their abuse and the heaping of insult upon injury is excessive. The young ladies have strayed as far from the natural path of affection as the young lords did at the beginning, and so will be denied for a while a thorough understanding and loving of their lords, not realizing at this moment that they are working against time and the fateful message of death.

The ladies leave and the men reappear, led by the

King. Boyet, more pretentious than usual in his manner, continues the game of deceit and humiliation that the girls began. Berowne's attitude after Boyet's exit, expressed in lines 316–335, and the King's reply make it clear that they are all put off by Boyet. They are disturbed by his airs and feel that he is the barrier between them and the ladies.

The ladies come back with great assurance, aplomb and formality. The men abandon their previous hesitations and bring out their most flowery and apologetic phrases, but the Princess and Rosaline proceed to bring them crashing down to reality. It is a funny scene, but has a slightly harsh edge to it. The men are offering love in a very innocent, direct way, and it is cruel of the girls to toy with their openhearted affection in so punitive a manner. The King is confused and put off by having the Princess twist his words, but he persists in his attempts at persuasion until the Princess says, "A mess of Russians left us but of late" (362). The men react with vivid interest about the Russians, and it would seem that the Princess, in her next lines ("Ay, in truth, my lord;/ Trim gallants, full of courtship and of state." [363–364]), is beginning to soften and repent. But Rosaline jumps in, and in her usual impetuous and overcompetitive manner, throws a few unnecessary darts. Berowne cannot leave her unchallenged, but Rosaline, playing from strength, outdoes him by far. The King soon gleans that the ladies know their secret and are now patronizing them, but Berowne won't give up and Rosaline won't let him. She squeezes the last ounce of fun from his embarrassment. Berowne finally seems to acknowledge defeat, but still using his wit and his tongue, he tries to retain a vestige of dignity with a torrent of words—an effort to outtalk and outcharm Rosaline. He begs for mercy but she is unrelenting.

Berowne then observes that since the ladies are wearing their tokens, they are not totally immune to the attentions of their various lovers. The boys want to be taken seriously—they no longer care to continue in the game-playing—but the girls still mock them. Berowne finally gives up: "Speak for yourselves," he says. "My wit is at an end" (431). And the King says, "Teach us, sweet madam, for our rude transgression/ Some fair excuse" (432–433). This is the moment toward which the ladies have been driving—unconditional surrender. They seem to have won. They have humbled the men and brought them to their knees.

The girls reveal how they fooled the men during the Russian disguise scene, and Berowne gradually realizes that they were given away by Boyet. The men begin to close in on Boyet and focus their anger and frustration on him. As the scene seems about to erupt into a violent and abrasive action—the men are feeling embarrassed and betrayed and the women are not offering any sweet conciliation—Costard bustles in, and the tone of the scene changes abruptly. His arrival is just in time; the chagrin of the lords and the superior position that the ladies have taken are dissipated in the common enjoyment of Costard and anticipation of the fun ahead. At first the King is fearful lest they further compound their position and says, "Berowne, they will shame us. Let them not approach," to which Berowne replies, "We are shameproof, my lord." The King insists: "I say they shall not come" (509 ff.). But the Princess overrules him with gentle persuasion, and one feels she is finally satisfied that the King has learned his lesson.

The nobles assemble to watch the show, which Armado introduces. This section creates an outrageous, farcical atmosphere that is a prelude and set-up for the news of the death of the King of France. It is necessary

for the director to watch the tone of the antic presentation so that the nobles do not become unpleasant or
seem unfeeling in their joking and condescension toward the "Worthies" and their entertainment. All their
interruptions must be in the spirit of good fun. For
instance, the comic character that is most dangerous
to deal with is Holofernes. He is severely drubbed and
insulted on stage. If it were not for the fact that he is
excessively pompous earlier and subjects other characters to his own brand of officious and pedantic put-
down, one might feel greater pity for him when he is
so abruptly thrust from the play. Note that, in spite of
the debacle, Holofernes does have the last word: "This
is not generous, not gentle, not humble" (621). And
he retires, wrapping his wounded dignity around him.

Some of the allusions and exchanges in the "antic"
are difficult to understand, but the spirit of the performance is not.

When the merriment is at its height and all the rustic
characters have had their comeuppance, the messenger,
Monsieur Marcade, enters, and the whole feeling and
tone of the scene and the play change with just two
sentences: "The king your father—", and the Princess
finishes the messenger's line: "Dead, for my life!"
(709–710). I got the sense, as in life, of a sudden,
chance event, which abruptly shifts life's course and
directs a person on a different and unpredicted path.
Berowne tells the Worthies to depart, and the stage,
which was filled with activity and motion and fun,
seems to dissolve as the Worthies and the footmen
quietly disappear. All that remains are the principal
characters and Boyet, who, upon hearing of the King's
death, sits in despair and shock on the edge of the fountain. All the men are now concerned, as are the women,
for the Princess and her well-being. But the Princess
immediately goes into action. You actually see her

assume a Queen's power as she says, "Boyet, prepare. I will away to-night" (717), and Boyet goes off to make the preparations.

The arrival scene is almost duplicated. By torch light and lantern light, servants upstage carry off trunks and other baggage to an awaiting conveyance offstage. Thus, the rather poignant partings of the various couples take place against the flurry and silent activity that physicalize A Departure. The ladies are brought coats made of chiffon material, which would be caught by the breeze. And suddenly one saw they were vulnerable and fragile creatures. I wanted to complement the atmosphere by contrasting the highly decorative surface glitter of their costumes (heightened by the flimsiness of the chiffon) to the very grim reality of death and the sadness of missed opportunities.

The King does his best to both comfort the Princess and argue his love but, as usual, expresses himself poorly and rather convolutedly. Berowne, the master of words, intervenes and tries to tell the Princess what they feel: "Honest plain words best pierce the ear of grief" (743). And at long last we have a Berowne who understands what words are for, who finds that they can communicate simply and directly and need not be used only as an instrument to falsify or mislead or manipulate. He pleads the men's cause as straightforwardly and beautifully as possible. The Princess answers with a speech that I think reveals the proper action of the play and expresses its theme: "We have received your letters, full of love," she starts, "And . . . rated them/ At courtship, pleasant jest, and courtesy,/ As bombast and as lining to the time./ But more devout than this in our respects/ Have we not been, and therefore met your loves/ In their own fashion, like a merriment" (767 ff.).

The King rejoins, a few lines later, "Now, at the

latest minute of the hour,/ Grant us your loves" (777–
778). And the Princess replies, "A time, methinks, too
short/ To make a world-without-end bargain in" (778–
779). And they proceed to make other bargains.

I tried to convey the feeling that each character had
in effect grown up, and that this experience they had
shared together had sobered them and changed them,
not for the moment, but forever—they were no longer
unable to experience love as a mature experience. There
is still a gentle and jocular quality in some of these
parting scenes, but underneath is a much deeper and
more sincere understanding, particularly on the part of
the men. After each couple exchanges their bargains,
they go to a different part of the stage to be alone and
give the next couple a sense of privacy. The last to deal
with their problems, and the ones most reluctant to
make a bargain are, of course, Berowne and his Rosaline.
But even he faces up to it, although Rosaline drives a
hard bargain. In keeping with Berowne's failings, she
makes him promise to use his words and his sense of
language to make the sick laugh, if he can, believing
that this will teach him a greater commitment to other
people.

As the ladies are about to leave, Armado suggests that
they watch the final pantomime that has been prepared.
The King, wanting to prolong the departure, grants his
permission. The rustics and the footmen come out onto
the two towers; one tower represents Hiems, the Winter, and the other Ver, the Spring. They begin the
song, "When daisies pied and violets blue . . ." (883).
Armado, in love with love, sits on the fountain in a
rhapsodic trance, eyes closed.

As the song progresses, Boyet enters to hurry the
ladies along, as if their carriage were waiting and ready
to go. The ladies slip out silently so as not to disrupt

the entertainment, each with her separate partner, until the stage is finally emptied of all but Armado, Rosaline, and Berowne.

Rosaline and Berowne still have not made up; they are sitting together during the entertainment, but back to back. And just as Rosaline is about to slip her hand into Berowne's and make the first gesture of reconciliation, Boyet quietly taps her on the shoulder, insisting that she come with him. She starts off and reaches the edge of the stage, but impulsively runs back to give Berowne a kiss. He is transformed by this one, simple act and runs after her, and the two of them come together in the first sentimental, romantic gesture that they have allowed themselves in the play. They disappear into the night, leaving only one singer singing the final, wistful scrap of tune: "Tu-whit, tu-who: a merry note,/ While greasy Joan doth keel the pot" (917–918). Finally even the singer drifts off, and only Armado is left.

Armado slowly opens his eyes to realize that all have gone and left him there alone. He looks at the audience and wistfully concludes, "The words of Mercury are harsh after the songs of Apollo," and, still addressing the audience, he says, "You, that way: we, this way. *Exeunt omnes*" (919–920). And as he leaves, the stage darkens and the play is over.

NEW YORK SHAKESPEARE FESTIVAL

DELACORTE THEATER, CENTRAL PARK, NEW YORK, SUMMER 1965

Produced by JOSEPH PAPP

IN COOPERATION WITH THE CITY OF NEW YORK
HON. ROBERT F. WAGNER, *Mayor*
HON. NEWBOLD MORRIS, *Commissioner of Parks*

PRESENTS WILLIAM SHAKESPEARE'S

LOVE'S LABOR'S LOST

Directed by GERALD FREEDMAN   Setting by MING CHO LEE
Lighting by MARTIN ARONSTEIN   Costumes by THEONI V. ALDREDGE
Songs and Music by JOHN MORRIS

THE CAST
(In order of speaking)

FERDINAND, *King of Navarre* .... James Ray
LONGAVILLE, *Lord attending on King* . . . Michael Moriarty
DUMAINE, *Lord attending on King* ...... William Bogert
BEROWNE, *Lord attending on King* ...... Richard Jordan
ANTHONY DULL, *a constable* .... Dan Durning
COSTARD, *a country swain* .... Joseph Bova
DON ADRIANO DE ARMADO,
   a fantastical Spaniard .... Paul Stevens
MOTH, *page to Don Adriano de Armado* .... John Pleshette
JAQUENETTA, *a country wench* .... Alexandra Berlin
BOYET, *Lord attending on Princess* .... Tom Aldredge
PRINCESS OF FRANCE .... Jane White
MARIA, *Lady attending on Princess* .... Nancy Reardon
KATHARINE, *Lady attending on Princess* . . . Margaret Linn
ROSALINE, *Lady attending on Princess* .... Rae Allen
A FORESTER .... Robert Burgess
SIR NATHANIEL, *a parson* .... Gerald E. McGonagill
HOLOFERNES, *a schoolmaster* .... Robert Ronan
MARCADE, *Lord attending on Princess* ...... Oliver Dixon
SINGER .... Keith Baker
DANCER .... Gerald Teijelo
LADY IN WAITING .... Betty Hellman
Attendants and Lords: Keith Baker, Robert Burgess, Burke
Byrnes, Oliver Dixon, John Hoffmeister, Peter Jacob, Bruce
Monette, John Vidette.

SCENE: NAVARRE
There will be one fifteen-minute intermission
Dance by Robert Joffrey
Associate Producer—BERNARD GERSTEN

Opening of Play
(I.i.) Upper left cupola: Navarre. Left to right (with rackets):
Longaville, Berowne, Dumaine. Pages (servants)

Berowne. "Necessity will make us all forsworn
   Three thousand times within this three years' space."
*(I.i.146–47) Left to right: Longaville, Berowne (sitting), Navarre,
Page (kneeling), Dumaine*

Berowne. "Now step I forth to whip hypocrisy.
    Ah, good my liege, I pray thee pardon me."
(IV.iii.146–47) *Top to bottom: Berowne, Navarre, Longaville,
Dumaine*

Berowne. "And when Love speaks, the voice of all the gods
 Make heaven drowsy with the harmony."
(IV.iii.339–340) Left to right: Dumaine, Longaville, Navarre, Berowne

Rosaline. "I am compared to twenty thousand fairs.
O, he hath drawn my picture in his letter!"
(V.ii.37–38) Left to right: Princess, Maria (standing), Rosaline, Katharine

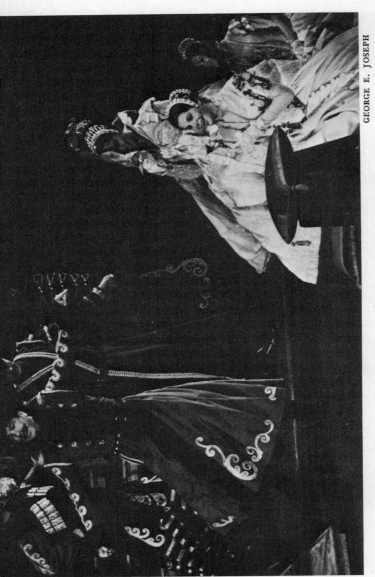

Russian Divertissement
(V.ii.) *Navarre (dancer in foreground), Princess and Rosaline (in foreground, left to right)*

GEORGE E. JOSEPH

GEORGE E. JOSEPH

Song. "When daisies pied and violets blue
And lady-smocks all silver-white. . . ."
(V.ii.883–84) *Armado (sitting on fountain) and Company*

Song. "And birds sit brooding in the snow,
        And Marian's nose looks red and raw. . . ."
(V.ii.912–13) Left to right: Armado, Berowne, Rosaline

THE FESTIVAL SHAKESPEARE

Love's Labor's Lost

A Note on the Text

The present edition, based on the 1598 Quarto and modified slightly in accord with the folio copy and scholarly tradition, contains a complete text of the play. Passages enclosed in parentheses were omitted from the New York Shakespeare Festival production. Stage directions or other passages set off by brackets are editorial additions to the original text. They have been handed down by successive editors. An asterisk following a word indicates that a production note pertaining to that passage may be found in the section entitled "Director's Preparation and Production Notes."

Love's Labor's Lost

ACT I. i

[*The park of the King of Navarre.*]

*Enter Ferdinand King of Navarre, Berowne, Longa-
ville, and Dumaine.*

KING. Let fame, that all hunt after in their lives,
Live regist'red upon our brazen tombs
And then grace us in the disgrace of death;
When, spite of cormorant devouring time,
Th' endeavor of this present breath may buy   5
That honor which shall bate his scythe's keen edge
And make us heirs of all eternity.
Therefore, brave conquerors, for so you are
That war against your own affections
And the huge army of the world's desires—   10
Our late edict shall strongly stand in force:
Navarre shall be the wonder of the world;
Our court shall be a little academe,
Still and contemplative in living art.
You three, Berowne, Dumaine, and Longaville,   15
Have sworn for three years' term to live with me,
My fellow scholars, and to keep those statutes
That are recorded in this schedule here.
Your oaths are passed; and now subscribe your names,

I.i.4 *cormorant* voracious   5 *present breath* living present   6 *bate
his* blunt its, i.e., time's   13 *academe* academy   14 *Still . . . art*
quiet and meditative in the art of living well

That his own hand may strike his honor down   20
That violates the smallest branch herein.
If you are armed to do, as sworn to do,
Subscribe to your deep oaths, and keep it too.
LONGAVILLE. I am resolved. 'Tis but a three years' fast.
The mind shall banquet though the body pine.   2
Fat paunches have lean pates, and dainty bits
Make rich the ribs, but bankrupt quite the wits.
DUMAINE. My loving lord, Dumaine is mortified.
The grosser manner of these world's delights
He throws upon the gross world's baser slaves.   3
To love, to wealth, to pomp, I pine and die,
With all these living in philosophy.*
BEROWNE. I can but say their protestation over;
So much, dear liege, I have already sworn,
That is, to live and study here three years.   3
But there are other strict observances:
As not to see a woman in that term,*
Which I hope well is not enrollèd there;
And one day in a week to touch no food,
And but one meal on every day beside,   4
The which I hope is not enrollèd there;
And then to sleep but three hours in the night,
And not be seen to wink of all the day,
When I was wont to think no harm all night
And make a dark night too of half the day,   4
Which I hope well is not enrollèd there.
O, these are barren tasks, too hard to keep,
Not to see ladies, study, fast, not sleep.
KING. Your oath is passed to pass away from these.*
BEROWNE. Let me say no, my liege, an if you please.   5
I only swore to study with your Grace
And stay here in your court for three years' space. .

20 *hand* signature   28 *mortified* dead to sensual pleasures   32 *all
these* King, Berowne, Longaville(?) love, wealth, pomp(?)   43
wink of all the day doze at all during the day   44 *wont to think
no harm* used to sleeping innocently, i.e., untroubled   50 *an if* if;
so found throughout Shakespeare's plays

LONGAVILLE. You swore to that, Berowne, and to the
  rest.
BEROWNE. By yea and nay, sir, then I swore in jest.
  What is the end of study, let me know?   55
KING. Why, that to know which else we should not know.
BEROWNE. Things hid and barred, you mean, from com-
  mon sense?
KING. Ay, that is study's godlike recompense.
BEROWNE. Come on then, I will swear to study so,
  To know the thing I am forbid to know: 60
  As thus—to study where I well may dine
  When I to feast expressly am forbid;
  Or study where to meet some mistress fine
  When mistresses from common sense are hid;
  Or having sworn too hard-a-keeping oath,   65
  Study to break it, and not break my troth.
  If study's gain be thus, and this be so,
  Study knows that which yet it doth not know.
  Swear me to this, and I will ne'er say no.
KING. These be the stops that hinder study quite,   70
  And train our intellects to vain delight.
BEROWNE. Why, all delights are vain, but that most vain
  Which, with pain purchased, doth inherit pain:
  As, painfully to pore upon a book,
  To seek the light of truth, while truth the while   75
  Doth falsely blind the eyesight of his look.
  Light seeking light, doth light of light beguile;
  So, ere you find where light in darkness lies,
  Your light grows dark by losing of your eyes.
  Study me how to please the eye indeed,   80
  By fixing it upon a fairer eye,
  Who dazzling so, that eye shall be his heed,
  And give him light that it was blinded by.

---

57 *common sense* ordinary perception   71 *train* entice   76 *falsely*
treacherously   77 *light . . . beguile* sight seeking truth does eyes of
sight cheat   80–84 *study . . . blinded by* study instead how to
please the eye truly, by fixing it, i.e., the eye, upon a fairer eye,
i.e., the eye of a lady, which is so dazzling that her eye shall become a guide and give light to the very eye it blinded

Study is like the heaven's glorious sun,
That will not be deep-searched with saucy looks: 85
Small have continual plodders ever won,
Save base authority from others' books.
These earthly godfathers of heaven's lights,
That give a name to every fixèd star,
Have no more profit of their shining nights   90
Than those that walk and wot not what they are.
Too much to know is to know nought but fame;
And every godfather can give a name.

KING. How well he's read to reason against reading!

DUMAINE. Proceeded well, to stop all good proceeding!   95

LONGAVILLE. He weeds the corn, and still lets grow the
    weeding.

BEROWNE. The spring is near, when green geese are
    a-breeding.

DUMAINE. How follows that?

BEROWNE.   Fit in his place and time.

DUMAINE. In reason nothing.

BEROWNE.   Something then in rime.

KING. Berowne is like an envious sneaping frost   100
That bites the first-born infants of the spring.

BEROWNE. Well, say I am; why should proud summer
    boast
Before the birds have any cause to sing?
Why should I joy in an abortive birth?
At Christmas I no more desire a rose   105
Than wish a snow in May's new-fangled shows;
But like of each thing that in season grows.
So you, to study now it is too late,
Climb o'er the house to unlock the little gate.

KING. Well, sit you out. Go home, Berowne. Adieu.   110

---

88 *earthly godfathers* i.e., the astronomers   91 *wot* know   93 *every
. . . name* i.e., at baptism   95 *Proceeded* has taken a degree at the
university   96 *weeding* weeds   97 *green geese* geese, bred upon
green grass, called spring geese, hence young and foolish   98 *Fit in
his* just in its   100 *sneaping* nipping, pinching   101 *infants* buds
108 *it is too late* you are too old

BEROWNE. No, my good lord, I have sworn to stay with
   you.
   And though I have for barbarism spoke more
   Than for that angel knowledge you can say,
   Yet confident I'll keep what I have swore,
   And bide the penance of each three years' day.   115
   Give me the paper, let me read the same,
   And to the strictest decrees I'll write my name.
KING. How well this yielding rescues thee from shame!
BEROWNE. [*reads*] "Item. That no woman shall come
   within a mile of my court—" Hath this been pro-
   claimed?   120
LONGAVILLE. Four days ago.
BEROWNE. Let's see the penalty. "—on pain of losing
   her tongue." Who devised this penalty?
LONGAVILLE. Marry, that did I.
BEROWNE.   Sweet lord, and why?
LONGAVILLE. To fright them hence with that dread
   penalty.   125
BEROWNE. A dangerous law against gentility!
   "Item. If any man be seen to talk with a woman
   within the term of three years, he shall endure such
   public shame as the rest of the court can possibly
   devise."
   This article, my liege, yourself must break;   130
   For well you know here comes in embassy
   The French king's daughter with yourself to speak,
   A maid of grace and complete majesty,
   About surrender up of Aquitaine
   To her decrepit, sick, and bed-rid father.   135
   Therefore this article is made in vain,
   Or vainly comes th' admirèd princess hither.
KING. What say you, lords? why, this was quite forgot.
BEROWNE. So study evermore is overshot.
   While it doth study to have what it would,   140

112 *barbarism* ignorance   115 *each three years' day* each day of
the three years   124 *Marry* by the Virgin Mary; so found throughout Shakespeare's plays   126 *gentility* polite behavior

It doth forget to do the thing it should;
And when it hath the thing it hunteth most,
'Tis won as towns with fire; so won, so lost.
KING. We must of force dispense with this decree;
  She must lie here on mere necessity.   145
BEROWNE. Necessity will make us all forsworn
  Three thousand times within this three years' space:
  For every man with his affects is born,
  Not by might mast'red, but by special grace.
  If I break faith, this word shall speak for me,   150
  I am forsworn "on mere necessity."
  So to the laws at large I write my name;
  And he that breaks them in the least degree
  Stands in attainder of eternal shame.
  Suggestions are to other as to me: 155
  But I believe, although I seem so loath,
  I am the last that will last keep his oath.
  But is there no quick recreation granted?
KING. Ay, that there is. Our court you know is haunted
  With a refinèd traveller of Spain,   160
  A man in all the world's new fashion planted,
  That hath a mint of phrases in his brain;
  One who the music of his own vain tongue
  Doth ravish like enchanting harmony;
  A man of complements, whom right and wrong   165
  Have chose as umpire of their mutiny.
  This child of fancy, that Armado hight,
  For interim to our studies shall relate
  In high-born words the worth of many a knight
  From tawny Spain, lost in the world's debate.   170

143 *with fire* with being burned down   144 *of force* perforce, i.e.,
forced by conditions   145 *lie* stay   148 *affects* passions   149 *Not
. . . mast'red* which are not controlled by his own power   149 *special grace* God's dispensation   154 *in attainder of* dishonored by
155 *suggestions* temptations   158 *quick* lively   159–60 *haunted
With* frequented by   165 *complements* ceremonious niceties   167
hight is named   168 *interim* interlude   170 *tawny Spain* Spain of
dark-skinned people(?) Spain of the dark soil(?)   170 *debate* war-
fare

How you delight, my lords, I know not, I;
But, I protest, I love to hear him lie,
And I will use him for my minstrelsy.
BEROWNE. Armado is a most illustrious wight,
A man of fire-new words, fashion's own knight.   175
LONGAVILLE. Costard the swain and he shall be our sport,
And so to study three years is but short.

*Enter [Dull,] a Constable with Costard with a
letter.**

CONSTABLE. Which is the duke's own person?
BEROWNE. This, fellow. What wouldst?
CONSTABLE. I myself reprehend his own person, for I am   180
his Grace's farborough: But I would see his own per-
son in flesh and blood.
BEROWNE. This is he.
CONSTABLE. Signior Arm—Arm—commends you. There's
villainy abroad. This letter will tell you more.   185
COSTARD. Sir, the contempts thereof are as touching me.
KING. A letter from the magnificent Armado.
BEROWNE. How low soever the matter, I hope in God
for high words.
LONGAVILLE. A high hope for a low heaven. God grant   190
us patience!
BEROWNE. To hear, or forbear hearing?
LONGAVILLE. To hear meekly, sir, and to laugh moder-
ately, or to forbear both.
BEROWNE. Well, sir, be it as the style shall give us cause   195
to climb in the merriness.
COSTARD. The matter is to me, sir, as concerning Jaque-
netta.
The manner of it is, I was taken with the manner.
BEROWNE. In what manner?

173 *minstrelsy* entertainer(?) entertainment(?)   175 *fire-new* brand-
ew   176 *swain* peasant or herdsman   180 *reprehend* (Dull is a
malaprop; he means "represent")   181 *farborough* (lisping approx-
mation of "thirdborough," a minor constable)   186 *contempts*
i.e., contents   197 *is to* concerns   198 *with the manner* in the act

COSTARD. In manner and form following, sir; all those   ₂₀₀
three. I was seen with her in the manor-house, sitting
with her upon the form, and taken following her into
the park; which, put together, is, in manner and form
following. Now, sir, for the manner—it is the manner
of a man to speak to a woman. For the form—in some   ₂₀₅
form.

BEROWNE. For the following, sir?

COSTARD. As it shall follow in my correction, and God
defend the right!

KING. Will you hear this letter with attention?

BEROWNE. As we would hear an oracle.   ₂₁₀

COSTARD. Such is the simplicity of man to hearken after
the flesh.

KING. [*reads*] "Great deputy, the welkin's vicegerent, and
sole dominator of Navarre, my soul's earth's God, and
body's fostering patron."   ₂₁₅

COSTARD. Not a word of Costard yet.

KING. "So it is—"

COSTARD. It may be so; but if he say it is so, he is, in
telling true, but so.

KING. Peace!   ₂₂₀

COSTARD. Be to me and every man that dares not fight.

KING. No words!

COSTARD. Of other men's secrets, I beseech you.

KING. "So it is, besieged with sable-colored melancholy, I
did commend the black-oppressing humor to the most   ₂₂
wholesome physic of thy health-giving air; and, as I am
a gentleman, betook myself to walk. The time when?
About the sixth hour, when beasts most graze, birds
best peck, and men sit down to that nourishment
which is called supper: So much for the time when.   ₂₃
Now for the ground which? which, I mean, I walked
upon: it is ycleped thy park. Then for the place
where? where, I mean, I did encounter that obscene

---

202 *form* bench   207 *correction* punishment   213 *welkin's vice-gerent* heaven's deputy   219 *but so* not worth much   232 *ycleped* called

and most preposterous event, that draweth from my
snow-white pen the ebon-colored ink, which here thou   235
viewest, beholdest, surveyest, or seest. But to the place
where? It standeth north-north-east and by east from
the west corner of thy curious-knotted garden. There
did I see that low-spirited swain, that base minnow of
thy mirth—"

COSTARD. Me?   240

KING. "that unlettered small-knowing soul—"

COSTARD. Me?

KING. "that shallow vassal—"

COSTARD. Still me?

KING. "which, as I remember, hight Costard—"   245

COSTARD. O me!

KING. "sorted and consorted, contrary to thy established
proclaimed edict and continent canon, which with—
O, with—but with this I passion to say wherewith—"

COSTARD. With a wench.   250

KING. "with a child of our grandmother Eve, a female;
or, for thy more sweet understanding, a woman. Him
I, as my ever-esteemed duty pricks me on, have sent
to thee, to receive the meed of punishment, by thy
sweet Grace's officer, Anthony Dull, a man of good   255
repute, carriage, bearing, and estimation."

DULL. Me, an 't shall please you; I am Anthony Dull.

KING. "For Jaquenetta, so is the weaker vessel called,
which I apprehended with the aforesaid swain, I keep
her as a vessel of thy law's fury; and shall, at the least   260
of thy sweet notice, bring her to trial. Thine in all
compliments of devoted and heart-burning heat of
duty,
        Don Adriano de Armado."

BEROWNE. This is not so well as I looked for, but the
best that ever I heard.   265

238 *curious-knotted* intricately arranged   239 *low-spirited* common   243 *vassal* lowly creature   245 *hight* is named   247 *sorted*
associated   248 *continent canon* law prescribing abstinence   249
passion grieve

KING. Ay, the best for the worst. But, sirrah, what say
  you to this?

COSTARD. Sir, I confess the wench.

KING. Did you hear the proclamation?

COSTARD. I do confess much of the hearing it, but little 27
  of the marking of it.

KING. It was proclaimed a year's imprisonment to be
  taken with a wench.

COSTARD. I was taken with none, sir; I was taken with a
  damsel.   27

KING. Well, it was proclaimed "damsel."

COSTARD. This was no damsel neither, sir; she was a
  virgin.

KING. It is so varied too, for it was proclaimed "virgin."

COSTARD. If it were, I deny her virginity; I was taken
  with a maid.   28

KING. This maid will not serve your turn, sir.

COSTARD. This maid will serve my turn, sir.

KING. Sir, I will pronounce your sentence: you shall fast
  a week with bran and water.

COSTARD. I had rather pray a month with mutton and   28
  porridge.

KING. And Don Armado shall be your keeper.
  My Lord Berowne, see him delivered o'er:
  And go we, lords, to put in practice that
  Which each to other hath so strongly sworn.   29
            [Exeunt King, Longaville, and Dumaine.]

BEROWNE. I'll lay my head to any good man's hat,
  These oaths and laws will prove an idle scorn.
  Sirrah, come on.

COSTARD. I suffer for the truth, sir; for true it is I was

266 *best . . . worst* the best example of the worst that can be found
266 *sirrah* (form of address to an inferior)   278 *It is so varied too*
this variation of damsel is specified too   281–82 *This maid . . .
my turn, sir* (1) King means that using the word maid will not help
Costard escape punishment (2) Costard asserts that the maid will
satisfy his purpose   285–86 *mutton and porridge* mutton-broth;
with quibble on "mutton," i.e., loose woman

taken with Jaquenetta, and Jaquenetta is a true girl;   295
and therefore welcome the sour cup of prosperity,
affliction may one day smile again, and till then sit
thee down, sorrow!

> *Exeunt.**

✦§ I. ii* §✦

Enter Armado, [a Braggart,] and Moth, his Page.

ARMADO.* Boy, what sign is it when a man of great spirit
grows melancholy?

MOTH. A great sign, sir, that he will look sad.*

ARMADO. Why, sadness is one and the selfsame thing,
dear imp.   5

MOTH. No, no, O Lord, sir, no!

ARMADO. How canst thou part sadness and melancholy,
my tender juvenal?

MOTH. By a familiar demonstration of the working, my
tough signor.   10

ARMADO. Why tough signor? why tough signor?

MOTH. Why tender juvenal? why tender juvenal?

ARMADO. I spoke it, tender juvenal, as a congruent
epitheton appertaining to thy young days, which we
may nominate tender.   15

MOTH. And I, tough signor, as an appertinent title to
your old time, which we may name tough.

ARMADO. Pretty, and apt.

MOTH. How mean you, sir? I pretty, and my saying apt?
or I apt, and my saying pretty?   20

ARMADO. Thou pretty, because little.

MOTH. Little pretty, because little. Wherefore apt?

ARMADO. And therefore apt, because quick.

---

297 *sit thee down* (proverbial; repeated IV.iii.4)   I.ii.7 *part* separate   8 *juvenal* youth   10 *signor* (quibble on "senior")   13–14
congruent epitheton suitable epithet   16 *an appertinent title* a
title belonging

MOTH. Speak you this in my praise, master?

ARMADO. In thy condign praise.   25

MOTH. I will praise an eel with the same praise.

ARMADO. What, that an eel is ingenious?

MOTH. That an eel is quick.

ARMADO. I do say thou art quick in answers. Thou
heat'st my blood.   30

MOTH. I am answered, sir.

ARMADO. I love not to be crossed.

MOTH. [aside] He speaks the mere contrary—crosses love
not him.

ARMADO. I have promised to study three years with the
duke.   35

MOTH. You may do it in an hour, sir.

ARMADO. Impossible.

MOTH. How many is one thrice told?

ARMADO. I am ill at reckoning; it fitteth the spirit of a
tapster.   40

MOTH. You are a gentleman and a gamester, sir.

ARMADO. I confess both. They are both the varnish of a
complete man.

MOTH. Then, I am sure you know how much the gross
sum of deuce-ace amounts to.   45

ARMADO. It doth amount to one more than two.

MOTH. Which the base vulgar do call three.

ARMADO. True.

MOTH. Why, sir, is this such a piece of study? Now here
is three studied ere ye'll thrice wink; and how easy it is   50
to put "years" to the word "three," and study three
years in two words, the dancing horse will tell you.

ARMADO. A most fine figure.

MOTH. [aside] To prove you a cipher.

ARMADO. I will hereupon confess I am in love; and as it   55

25 *condign* well-merited   33 *crosses* type of coins stamped with
crosses; pun was widespread   40 *tapster* bartender   42 *varnish*
polish   47 *vulgar* common people   52 *dancing horse* (the noted
trained horse, Morocco, owned by Master Banks, performed arith-
metical feats by tapping two dice, one marked ace, the other deuce)
53 *figure* i.e., of speech

is base for a soldier to love, so am I in love with a base
wench. If drawing my sword against the humor of affection would deliver me from the reprobate thought
of it, I would take Desire prisoner and ransom him to
any French courtier for a new devised curtsy. I think   60
scorn to sigh: methinks I should outswear Cupid.
Comfort me, boy. What great men have been in love?

MOTH. Hercules, master.

ARMADO. Most sweet Hercules! More authority, dear
boy, name more; and, sweet my child, let them be   65
men of good repute and carriage.

MOTH. Samson, master—he was a man of good carriage,
great carriage, for he carried the town-gates on his
back like a porter, and he was in love.

ARMADO. O well-knit Samson! strong-jointed Samson! I   70
do excel thee in my rapier as much as thou didst me
in carrying gates. I am in love too. Who was Samson's
love, my dear Moth?

MOTH. A woman, master.

ARMADO. Of what complexion?   75

MOTH. Of all the four, or the three, or the two, or one of
the four.

ARMADO. Tell me precisely of what complexion.

MOTH. Of the sea-water green, sir.

ARMADO. Is that one of the four complexions?   80

MOTH. As I have read, sir, and the best of them too.

ARMADO. Green indeed is the color of lovers; but to have
a love of that color, methinks Samson had small reason for it. He surely affected her for her wit.

MOTH. It was so, sir, for she had a green wit.   85

ARMADO. My love is most immaculate white and red.

MOTH. Most maculate thoughts, master, are masked
under such colors.

57–58 *humor of affection* disposition towards romantic passion   59–
60 *ransom him . . . curtsy* trade Desire to any French courtier for
one of the latest fads of bowing   60–61 *think scorn* disdain   61
outswear forswear   75 *complexion* (1)temperament (2)skin-color-
ing   84 *affected . . . wit* loved her for her mind   85 *green* im-
mature

ARMADO. Define, define, well-educated infant.

MOTH. My father's wit, and my mother's tongue, assist
    me! 90

ARMADO. Sweet invocation of a child, most pretty and
    pathetical.

MOTH. If she be made of white and red,
        Her faults will ne'er be known,
    For blushing cheeks by faults are bred, 95
        And fears by pale white shown;
    Then if she fear, or be to blame,
        By this you shall not know,
    For still her cheeks possess the same
        Which native she doth owe. 100
A dangerous rime, master, against the reason of white
and red.

ARMADO. Is there not a ballet, boy, of the King and the
    Beggar?

MOTH. The world was very guilty of such a ballet some 105
    three ages since; but I think now 'tis not to be found;
    or if it were, it would neither serve for the writing nor
    the tune.

ARMADO. I will have that subject newly writ o'er, that I
    may example my digression by some mighty prece-
    dent. Boy, I do love that country girl that I took in the 110
    park with the rational hind Costard. She deserves well.

MOTH. [aside] To be whipped; and yet a better love than
    my master.

ARMADO. Sing, boy. My spirit grows heavy in love.

MOTH. And that's great marvel, loving a light wench. 11

ARMADO. I say, sing.

MOTH. Forbear till this company be past.

---

92 *pathetical* touching   99–100 *For still . . . owe* for always her
cheeks keep the same coloring which naturally she possesses   103–
104 *ballet . . . Beggar* ballad, boy, of King Cophetua and the
beggar-maid whom he loved   107 *it would . . . writing* it would not
prove suitable for the lyrics   109 *digression* deviation (from my
soldierly behavior)   111 *rational hind* intelligent bumpkin

Enter [Costard, the] Clown, [Dull, the] Constable,
and [Jaquenetta, a] Wench.

DULL. Sir, the duke's pleasure is, that you keep Costard
safe, and you must suffer him to take no delight nor
no penance, but 'a must fast three days a week. For   120
this damsel, I must keep her at the park; she is allowed
for the day-woman. Fare you well.*

ARMADO. I do betray myself with blushing. Maid.

JAQUENETTA. Man.

ARMADO. I will visit thee at the lodge.   125

JAQUENETTA. That's hereby.

ARMADO. I know where it is situate.

JAQUENETTA. Lord, how wise you are!

ARMADO. I will tell thee wonders.

JAQUENETTA. With that face.   130

ARMADO. I love thee.

JAQUENETTA. So I heard you say.

ARMADO. And so farewell.

JAQUENETTA. Fair weather after you!

DULL. Come, Jaquenetta, away!   135

            Exeunt [Dull and Jaquenetta].

ARMADO. Villain, thou shalt fast for thy offenses ere thou
be pardoned.

COSTARD. Well, sir, I hope when I do it I shall do it on
a full stomach.

ARMADO. Thou shalt be heavily punished.   140

COSTARD. I am more bound to you than your fellows, for
they are but lightly rewarded.

ARMADO. Take away this villain. Shut him up.

MOTH. Come, you transgressing slave, away!

COSTARD. Let me not be pent up, sir. I will fast, being
loose.   145

---

120 *penance* perhaps a malaprop for "pleasance"(?)   120 *'a* he; so
found throughout Shakespeare's plays   121–22 *allowed . . . day-
woman* permitted to serve as the dairy-maid   130 *With that face*
(said caustically)   138–39 *on . . . stomach* (1) well-fed (2) bravely

MOTH. No, sir; that were fast and loose. Thou shalt to prison.

COSTARD. Well, if ever I do see the merry days of desolation that I have seen, some shall see—

MOTH. What shall some see?   150

COSTARD. Nay, nothing, Master Moth, but what they look upon. It is not for prisoners to be too silent in their words, and therefore I will say nothing. I thank God I have as little patience as another man, and therefore I can be quiet.

                              Exit [with Moth].

ARMADO. I do affect the very ground, which is base,   155
where her shoe, which is baser, guided by her foot, which is basest, doth tread. I shall be forsworn, which is a great argument of falsehood, if I love. And how can that be true love which is falsely attempted? Love is a familiar; Love is a devil. There is no evil angel but 160
Love. Yet was Samson so tempted, and he had an excellent strength; yet was Solomon so seduced, and he had a very good wit. Cupid's butt-shaft is too hard for Hercules' club, and therefore too much odds for a Spaniard's rapier. The first and second cause will not 165
serve my turn: the passado he respects not, the duello he regards not. His disgrace is to be called boy, but his glory is to subdue men. Adieu, valor! rust, rapier! be still, drum! for your manager is in love; yea, he loveth. Assist me some extemporal god of rime, for I 170
am sure I shall turn sonnet. Devise, wit! write, pen! for I am for whole volumes in folio.   *Exit.*

146 *fast and loose* (a game involving deception and trickery)   158
argument proof   160 *familiar* attendant devil or spirit   163 *butt-shaft* unbarbed arrow used for target practice   165 *first . . . cause* (precise justifications for undertaking duels as set down by authority)   166 *passado* thrust in fencing   166 *duello* the prescribed rules of duelling   169 *manager* one who manages, i.e., skillfully, the military arts   171 *turn sonnet* fashion sonnets(?) become the very personification of a sonnet(?)

⤳ II. i* ⤶

*Enter the Princess of France, with three attending
Ladies, [Rosaline, Maria, Katharine,] and three
Lords, [one of whom is Boyet].*

BOYET. Now, madam, summon up your dearest spirits.*
  Consider who the king your father sends,
  To whom he sends, and what's his embassy:
  Yourself, held precious in the world's esteem,
  To parley with the sole inheritor   5
  Of all perfections that a man may owe,
  Matcheless Navarre; the plea of no less weight
  Than Aquitaine, a dowry for a queen.
  Be now as prodigal of all dear grace
  As Nature was in making graces dear,   10
  When she did starve the general world beside,
  And prodigally gave them all to you.
PRINCESS. Good Lord Boyet, my beauty, though but
    mean,
  Needs not the painted flourish of your praise:
  Beauty is bought by judgment of the eye,   15
  Not uttered by base sale of chapmen's tongues.
  I am less proud to hear you tell my worth
  Than you much willing to be counted wise
  In spending your wit in the praise of mine.
  But now to task the tasker: good Boyet,   20
  You are not ignorant, all-telling fame
  Doth noise abroad, Navarre hath made a vow,
  Till painful study shall outwear three years,
  No woman may approach his silent court:

II.i.1 *dearest spirits* best wits   5 *inheritor* owner   6 *owe* own   14
flourish embellishment   16 *uttered* passed about   16 *chapmen's*
salesmen's   20 *task . . . tasker* give a task to the one who admon-
ishes me   23 *painful* painstaking   23 *outwear* outlast

Therefore to's seemeth it a needful course,   25
Before we enter his forbidden gates,
To know his pleasure; and in that behalf,
Bold of your worthiness, we single you
As our best-moving fair solicitor.
Tell him, the daughter of the King of France,   30
On serious business, craving quick dispatch,
Importunes personal conference with his Grace.
Haste, signify so much; while we attend,
Like humble-visaged suitors, his high will.
BOYET. Proud of employment, willingly I go.   35
                              Exit Boyet.
PRINCESS. All pride is willing pride, and yours is so.
Who are the votaries, my loving lords,
That are vow-fellows with this virtuous duke?
LORD. Longaville is one.
PRINCESS.   Know you the man?
MARIA. I know him, madam. At a marriage feast   40
Between Lord Perigort and the beauteous heir
Of Jacques Falconbridge solemnizèd
In Normandy saw I this Longaville.
A man of sovereign parts he is esteemed,
Well fitted in arts, glorious in arms: 45
Nothing becomes him ill that he would well.
The only soil of his fair virtue's gloss,
If virtue's gloss will stain with any soil,
Is a sharp wit matched with too blunt a will,
Whose edge hath power to cut, whose will still wills 50
It should none spare that come within his power.
PRINCESS. Some merry mocking lord, belike; is 't so?
MARIA. They say so most that most his humors know.
PRINCESS. Such short-lived wits do wither as they grow.
Who are the rest?   55

25 *to's* to us   28 *Bold* confident   29 *best-moving* most eloquent
37 *votaries* sworn adherents (to the studious and celibate life)
45 *fitted in arts* endowed with learning   46 *Nothing . . . well*
nothing is unsuitable to him that he wishes to do well   49 *blunt*
dull, insensitive   50 *Whose edge* i.e., of his wit

KATHARINE. The young Dumaine, a well-accomplished
        youth,
    Of all that virtue love for virtue loved;
    Most power to do most harm, least knowing ill,
    For he hath wit to make an ill shape good,
    And shape to win grace though he had no wit.   60
    I saw him at the Duke Alençon's once;
    And much too little of that good I saw
    Is my report to his great worthiness.
ROSALINE. Another of these students at that time
    Was there with him, if I have heard a truth.   65
    Berowne they call him; but a merrier man,
    Within the limit of becoming mirth,
    I never spent an hour's talk withal.
    His eye begets occasion for his wit;
    For every object that the one doth catch   70
    The other turns to a mirth-moving jest,
    Which his fair tongue, conceit's expositor,
    Delivers in such apt and gracious words,
    That agèd ears play truant at his tales,
    And younger hearings are quite ravishèd,   75
    So sweet and voluble is his discourse.
PRINCESS. God bless my ladies! Are they all in love,
    That every one her own hath garnishèd
    With such bedecking ornaments of praise?
LORD. Here comes Boyet.

        Enter Boyet.

PRINCESS.   Now, what admittance, lord?   80
BOYET. Navarre had notice of your fair approach;
    And he and his competitors in oath
    Were all addressed to meet you, gentle lady,

58–60 *Most . . . wit* best able to do the greatest evil, though he
knows evil least of any, because he has the wit to make an evil
appearance seem good and the physique to win admiration though
he were devoid of wit   70–71 *the one . . . The other* the eye doth
glance at, his wit   72 *conceit's* imagination's   74 *play truant* leave
hearing their proper, i.e., serious, subjects   76 *voluble* fluent   82
competitors partners   83 *addressed* ready

Before I came. Marry, thus much I have learnt;
He rather means to lodge you in the field,   85
Like one that comes here to besiege his court,
Than seek a dispensation for his oath
To let you enter his unpeopled house.

Enter Navarre, Longaville, Dumaine, and Berowne.

Here comes Navarre.
KING. Fair princess, welcome to the court of Navarre.   90
PRINCESS. "Fair" I give you back again, and "welcome"
    I have not yet. The roof of this court is too high to be
    yours, and welcome to the wide fields too base to be
    mine.
KING. You shall be welcome, madam, to my court.
PRINCESS. I will be welcome, then. Conduct me thither.   95
KING. Hear me, dear lady; I have sworn an oath.
PRINCESS. Our Lady help my lord! he'll be forsworn.
KING. Not for the world, fair madam, by my will.
PRINCESS. Why, will shall break it; will, and nothing else.
KING. Your ladyship is ignorant what it is.   100
PRINCESS. Were my lord so, his ignorance were wise,
    Where now his knowledge must prove ignorance.
    I hear your Grace hath sworn out house-keeping:
    'Tis deadly sin to keep that oath, my lord,
    And sin to break it.   105
    But pardon me, I am too sudden-bold:
    To teach a teacher ill beseemeth me.
    Vouchsafe to read the purpose of my coming,
    And suddenly resolve me in my suit.
KING. Madam, I will, if suddenly I may.   110
PRINCESS. You will the sooner that I were away,
    For you'll prove perjured if you make me stay.
BEROWNE. Did not I dance with you in Brabant once?
ROSALINE. Did not I dance with you in Brabant once?

---

88 *unpeopled* i.e., without servants   92 *roof . . . court* i.e., the
open sky   98 *by my will* willingly   103 *sworn out house-keeping*
sworn off hospitality   109 *suddenly* immediately   111 *You will
. . . away* you had better do it sooner so that I may leave(?)

BEROWNE. I know you did.

ROSALINE.   How needless was it then   115
  To ask the question!

BEROWNE.   You must not be so quick.

ROSALINE. 'Tis long of you that spur me with such questions.

BEROWNE. Your wit's too hot, it speeds too fast, 'twill
  tire.

ROSALINE. Not till it leave the rider in the mire.

BEROWNE. What time o' day?   120

ROSALINE. The hour that fools should ask.

BEROWNE. Now fair befall your mask!

ROSALINE. Fair fall the face it covers!

BEROWNE. And send you many lovers!

ROSALINE. Amen, so you be none.   125

BEROWNE. Nay, then will I be gone.

KING. Madam, your father here doth intimate
  The payment of a hundred thousand crowns;
  Being but the one half of an entire sum
  Disbursèd by my father in his wars.*   130
  But say that he, or we, as neither have,
  Received that sum, yet there remains unpaid
  A hundred thousand more; in surety of the which,
  One part of Aquitaine is bound to us,
  Although not valued to the money's worth.   135
  If then the king your father will restore
  But that one half which is unsatisfied,
  We will give up our right in Aquitaine,
  And hold fair friendship with his Majesty.
  But that, it seems, he little purposeth,   140
  For here he doth demand to have repaid
  A hundred thousand crowns; and not demands,
  On payment of a hundred thousand crowns,
  To have his title live in Aquitaine;

---

116 *quick* sharp   117 *long of* on account of   122 *fair befall* good
fortune on   127 *doth intimate* refers to   142 *and not demands*
rather than demanding

Which we much rather had depart withal,   145
And have the money by our father lent,
Than Aquitaine, so gelded as it is.
Dear princess, were not his requests so far
From reason's yielding, your fair self should make
A yielding 'gainst some reason in my breast,   150
And go well satisfied to France again.

PRINCESS. You do the king my father too much wrong,
And wrong the reputation of your name,
In so unseeming to confess receipt
Of that which hath so faithfully been paid.   155

KING. I do protest I never heard of it;
And if you prove it, I'll repay it back
Or yield up Aquitaine.

PRINCESS.   We arrest your word.
Boyet, you can produce acquittances
For such a sum from special officers   160
Of Charles his father.

KING.   Satisfy me so.

BOYET. So please your Grace, the packet is not come
Where that and other specialties are bound.
To-morrow you shall have a sight of them.

KING. It shall suffice me—at which interview   165
All liberal reason I will yield unto.
Meantime, receive such welcome at my hand
As honor, without breach of honor, may
Make tender of to thy true worthiness.
You may not come, fair princess, within my gates; 170
But here without you shall be so received
As you shall deem yourself lodged in my heart,
Though so denied fair harbor in my house.
Your own good thoughts excuse me, and farewell.
To-morrow shall we visit you again.   175

PRINCESS. Sweet health and fair desires consort your
     Grace.

---

145 *had depart withal* part with moreover   147 *gelded* devalued
154 *so unseeming* seeming not   158 *arrest your word* seize your
word as assurance   169 *Make tender of* offer   176 *consort* accompany

KING. Thy own wish wish I thee in every place.

 Exit [with Longaville and Dumaine].

BEROWNE. Lady, I will commend you to mine own heart.

ROSALINE. Pray you, do my commendations; I would be
 glad to see it.   180

BEROWNE. I would you heard it groan.

ROSALINE. Is the fool sick?

BEROWNE. Sick at the heart.

ROSALINE. Alack, let it blood.

BEROWNE. Would that do it good?   185

ROSALINE. My physic says "ay."

BEROWNE. Will you prick 't with your eye?

ROSALINE. No *point*, with my knife.*

BEROWNE. Now, God save thy life.

ROSALINE. And yours from long living.   190

BEROWNE. I cannot stay thanksgiving.   *Exit*

 Enter Dumaine.

DUMAINE. Sir, I pray you a word: what lady is that same?

BOYET. The heir of Alençon, Katharine her name.

DUMAINE. A gallant lady. Monsieur, fare you well.

 Exit.

 [Enter Longaville.]

LONGAVILLE. I beseech you a word: what is she in the
 white?   195

BOYET. A woman sometimes, an you saw her in the light.

LONGAVILLE. Perchance light in the light. I desire her
 name.

BOYET. She hath but one for herself; to desire that were
 a shame.

LONGAVILLE. Pray you, sir, whose daughter?

BOYET. Her mother's, I have heard.   200

---

184 *let it blood* bleed it, i.e., resort to bloodletting for a cure
188 *No point* not at all; negation borrowed from French with
quibble on "point"   196 *an* if; so found throughout Shakespeare's
plays   196 *in the light* in her true light(?) without a mask(?)
197 *light in the light* loose, i.e., wanton in the light

LONGAVILLE. God's blessing on your beard!
BOYET. Good sir, be not offended.

    She is an heir of Falconbridge.
LONGAVILLE. Nay, my choler is ended.

    She is a most sweet lady.   205
BOYET. Not unlike, sir; that may be.   *Exit Longaville.*

    Enter Berowne.

BEROWNE. What's her name, in the cap?
BOYET. Rosaline, by good hap.
BEROWNE. Is she wedded or no?
BOYET. To her will, sir, or so.   210
BEROWNE. You are welcome, sir. Adieu.
BOYET. Farewell to me, sir, and welcome to you.

                                     Exit Berowne.

MARIA. That last is Berowne, the merry madcap lord.

    Not a word with him but a jest.
BOYET.   And every jest but a word.
PRINCESS. It was well done of you to take him at his

    word.   215
BOYET. I was as willing to grapple as he was to board.
KATHARINE. Two hot sheeps, marry!
BOYET.   And wherefore not ships?

    No sheep, sweet lamb, unless we feed on your lips.
KATHARINE. You sheep and I pasture: shall that finish

    the jest?
BOYET. So you grant pasture for me.
KATHARINE.   Not so, gentle beast.   220

    My lips are no common, though several they be.
BOYET. Belonging to whom?
KATHARINE.   To my fortunes and me.

---

201 *blessing on your beard* (an insulting remark)   212 *Farewell
. . . you* (double-edged farewell suggesting that Berowne is glad to
get away and Boyet is glad to see him go)   215 *take . . . word*
answer him in his own way   217 *ships* ("ships" and "sheeps" had
the same pronunciation)   221 *My lips . . . they be* my lips are
not common pasture, though they are cultivated fields, privately
owned

PRINCESS. Good wits will be jangling; but, gentles, agree.
This civil war of wits were much better used
On Navarre and his book-men, for here 'tis abused.   225
BOYET. If my observation, which very seldom lies,
By the heart's still rhetoric disclosèd with eyes
Deceive me not now, Navarre is infected.
PRINCESS. With what?
BOYET. With that which we lovers entitle affected.   230
PRINCESS. Your reason.
BOYET. Why, all his behaviors did make their retire
To the court of his eye, peeping thorough desire.
His heart, like an agate, with your print impressèd,
Proud with his form, in his eye pride expressèd.   235
His tongue, all impatient to speak and not see,
Did stumble with haste in his eyesight to be;
All senses to that sense did make their repair,
To feel only looking on fairest of fair.
Methought all his senses were locked in his eye,   240
As jewels in crystal for some prince to buy;
Who, tend'ring their own worth from where they
were glassed,
Did point you to buy them, along as you passed.
His face's own margent did quote such amazes,
That all eyes saw his eyes enchanted with gazes.   245

225 *book-men* (scornfully) scholars   225 *abused* misplaced   227 *still rhetoric* silent eloquence   230 *affected* impassioned   232–33 *all his . . . desire* all his actions gathered together in the court of his eye, peering at you through a veil of love   234 *agate* (a variety of quartz into which figures were cut or impressed)   235 *his form* its form, i.e., the impressure of the Princess   236–37 *His tongue . . . eyesight to be* his tongue, extremely impatient with speaking and not seeing, stumbled over itself in its rush to become part of his eyesight   238–39 *All senses . . . fair* all of his senses to the sense of sight did resort (go), able to feel only through gazing upon the fairest woman of all   242 *Who, tend'ring* which, i.e., the senses and the jewels, setting forth   242 *from where* in the setting, i.e., the eye where   243 *point* urge   244 *margent* the illumination or commentary in the margin of a book   244 *amazes* admiration

I'll give you Aquitaine, and all that is his,
An you give him for my sake but one loving kiss.

PRINCESS. Come to our pavilion. Boyet is disposed.

BOYET. But to speak that in words which his eye hath
disclosed.*

I only have made a mouth of his eye,   250
By adding a tongue which I know will not lie.

ROSALINE. Thou art an old love-monger, and speakest
skilfully.

MARIA. He is Cupid's grandfather, and learns news of
him.

KATHARINE. Then was Venus like her mother, for her
father is but grim.

BOYET. Do you hear, my mad wenches?

ROSALINE.   No.

BOYET.   What, then, do you see?   255

ROSALINE. Ay, our way to be gone.

BOYET.   You are too hard for me.

                                        Exeunt omnes.

◦§ III. i §◦

Enter [Armado, the] Braggart, and [Moth,] his Boy.

ARMADO. Warble, child; make passionate my sense of
hearing.

MOTH. Concolinel.*

ARMADO. Sweet air! Go, tenderness of years, take this key,
give enlargement to the swain, bring him festinately   5
hither. I must employ him in a letter to my love.*

MOTH. Master, will you win your love with a French
brawl?

ARMADO. How meanest thou? Brawling in French?

---

248 *disposed* i.e., to be merry   252 *skilfully* knowingly   III.i.3
Concolinel a phonetic corruption of the title of an Irish song(?)
5 *festinately* quickly   7 *brawl* a French dance

MOTH.* No, my complete master; but to jig off a tune at
     the tongue's end, canary to it with your feet, humor   10
     it with turning up your eyelids, sigh a note and sing a
     note, sometime through the throat as if you swallowed
     love with singing love, sometime through the nose as
     if you snuffed up love by smelling love; with your hat
     penthouse-like o'er the shop of your eyes; with your   15
     arms crossed on your thin-belly doublet like a rabbit
     on a spit; or your hands in your pocket like a man
     after the old painting; and keep not too long in one
     tune, but a snip and away. These are complements,
     these are humors, these betray nice wenches (that   20
     would be betrayed without these), and make them
     men of note; do you note, men that most are affected
     to these.
ARMADO. How hast thou purchased this experience?
MOTH. By my penny of observation.
ARMADO. But O—but O—   25
MOTH. The hobby-horse is forgot.
ARMADO. Call'st thou my love "hobby-horse"?
MOTH. No, master; the hobby-horse is but a colt, and
     your love perhaps a hackney.* But have you forgot
     your love?
ARMADO. Almost I had.   30
MOTH. Negligent student! learn her by heart.
ARMADO. By heart, and in heart, boy.
MOTH. And out of heart, master. All those three I will
     prove.
ARMADO. What wilt thou prove?
MOTH. A man, if I live; and this, by, in, and without,   35
     upon the instant. By heart you love her, because your

10 *canary to it* dance to the tune; the canary was a lively Spanish
dance   15 *penthouse-like o'er the shop* a projection or overhang
over a door or shop   16 *thin-belly doublet* a doublet over a thin
belly(?) a doublet with little padding(?); both senses may be intended   20 *humors* caprices   22 *affected* inclined   25–26 *But O
. . . forgot* fragment of a popular ballad(?)   27–29 *hobby-horse,
hackney* a loose woman or prostitute

heart cannot come by her; in heart you love her, because your heart is in love with her; and out of heart
you love her, being out of heart that you cannot enjoy
her.

ARMADO. I am all these three.   40

MOTH. And three times as much more, and yet nothing
at all.

ARMADO. Fetch hither the swain. He must carry me a
letter.

MOTH. [aside] A message well sympathized—a horse to
be ambassador for an ass.   45

ARMADO. Ha, ha, what sayest thou?

MOTH. Marry, sir, you must send the ass upon the horse,
for he is very slow-gaited. But I go.

ARMADO. The way is but short. Away!

MOTH. As swift as lead, sir.   50

ARMADO. The meaning, pretty ingenious?
Is not lead a metal heavy, dull, and slow?

MOTH. Minime, honest, master; or rather, master, no.

ARMADO. I say, lead is slow.

MOTH.   You are too swift, sir, to say so.
Is that lead slow which is fired from a gun?   55

ARMADO. Sweet smoke of rhetoric!
He reputes me a cannon, and the bullet, that's he:
I shoot thee at the swain.

MOTH.   Thump, then, and I flee. [Exit.]

ARMADO. A most acute juvenal; voluble and free of grace!
By thy favor, sweet welkin, I must sigh in thy face: 60
Most rude melancholy, valor gives thee place.
My herald is returned.

    Enter [Moth, the] Page, and [Costard, the] Clown.

MOTH. A wonder, master! Here's a costard* broken in a
shin.

44 *sympathized* joined in harmony   53 *Minime* by no means   58
Thump boom, i.e., the cannon's sound   59 *acute juvenal* keen-
witted youngster   60 *welkin* sky   61 *gives thee place* gives way to
you   63 *costard* (1) large apple (2) head

ARMADO. Some enigma, some riddle. Come, thy *l'envoy*
   —begin.

COSTARD. No egma, no riddle, no *l'envoy*; no salve in the   65
   mail, sir. O, sir, plantain, a plain plantain. No *l'envoy*,
   no *l'envoy*, no salve, sir, but a plantain.

ARMADO. By virtue, thou enforcest laughter; thy silly
   thought, my spleen; the heaving of my lungs provokes
   me to ridiculous smiling. O, pardon me, my stars!   70
   Doth the inconsiderate take *salve* for *l'envoy*, and the
   word *l'envoy* for a salve?

MOTH. Do the wise think them other? Is not *l'envoy* a
   salve?

ARMADO. No, page; it is an epilogue, or discourse to
   make plain

Some obscure precedence that hath tofore been sain.   75
I will example it:
         The fox, the ape, and the humble-bee,
         Were still at odds, being but three.
There's the moral. Now the *l'envoy*.

MOTH. I will add the *l'envoy*. Say the moral again.   80

ARMADO. The fox, the ape, and the humble-bee,
         Were still at odds, being but three.

MOTH.   Until the goose came out of door,
         And stayed the odds by adding four.
Now will I begin your moral, and do you follow with   85
my *l'envoy*.
         The fox, the ape, and the humble-bee,
         Were still at odds, being but three.

ARMADO. Until the goose came out of door,
         Staying the odds by adding four.   90

---

64 *l'envoy* concluding comment to a prose or poetical composition
65–66 *No egma . . . mail* (Costard misinterprets enigma, riddle and
l'envoy, taking them to be types of salves, with a quibble on the
Latin *salve*, a salute, and stating he has no ointment in his wallet)
66 *plantain* (the leaf of the plantain was a popular remedy for
bruised shins)   69 *spleen* (here, the seat of laughter)   71 *inconsiderate* unlearned, i.e., ignorant fellow   75 *sain* spoken   84 *stayed*
eliminated   84 *four* a fourth   89 *goose* i.e., Armado

MOTH. A good *l'envoy*, ending in the goose. Would you
    desire more?

COSTARD. The boy hath sold him a bargain, a goose,
    that's flat.
    Sir, your pennyworth is good, an your goose be fat.
    To sell a bargain well is as cunning as fast and loose.*   95
    Let me see, a fat *l'envoy*; ay, that's a fat goose.

ARMADO. Come hither, come hither. How did this argu-
    ment begin?

MOTH. By saying that a costard was broken in a shin.
    Then called you for the *l'envoy*.

COSTARD. True, and I for a plantain; thus came your ar-   100
    gument in;
    Then the boy's fat *l'envoy*, the goose that you bought;
    And he ended the market.

ARMADO. But tell me, how was there a costard broken in
    a shin?

MOTH. I will tell you sensibly.   105

COSTARD. Thou hast no feeling of it, Moth. I will speak
    that *l'envoy*.
    I, Costard, running out, that was safely within,
    Fell over the threshold and broke my shin.

ARMADO. We will talk no more of this matter.   110

COSTARD. Till there be more matter in the shin.

ARMADO. Sirrah Costard, I will enfranchise thee.

COSTARD. O, marry me to one Frances! I smell some
    l'envoy, some goose, in this.

ARMADO. By my sweet soul, I mean setting thee at lib-   115
    erty, enfreedoming thy person. Thou wert immured,
    restrained, captivated, bound.

COSTARD. True, true, and now you will be my purgation
    and let me loose.

ARMADO. I give thee thy liberty, set thee from dur-   120
    ance; and in lieu thereof, impose on thee nothing

---

93 *sold . . . bargain* made a fool of him   94 *an* if   95 *fast and
loose* (a game involving deception and trickery)   105 *sensibly*
(1) in a sensible manner (2) with feeling   112 *enfranchise* liberate

but this. Bear this significant to the country maid
Jaquenetta. There is remuneration; for the best ward
of mine honor is rewarding my dependents. Moth,
follow.   [*Exit.*]   125
MOTH. Like the sequel, I. Signior Costard, adieu.   *Exit.*
COSTARD. My sweet ounce of man's flesh, my incony Jew!
  Now will I look to his remuneration.* Remuneration?
  O that's the Latin word for three farthings. Three
  farthings—remuneration. "What's the price of this   130
  inkle?" "One penny." "No, I'll give you a remuneration." Why, it carries it! Remuneration! Why, it is a
  fairer name than French crown. I will never buy and
  sell out of this word.

  Enter Berowne.

BEROWNE. O my good knave Costard, exceedingly well
    met.
COSTARD. Pray you, sir, how much carnation ribbon may   135
  a man buy for a remuneration?
BEROWNE. O, what is a remuneration?
COSTARD. Marry, sir, halfpenny farthing.
BEROWNE. O, why then, three-farthing-worth of silk.
COSTARD. I thank your worship. God be wi' you.   140
BEROWNE. O stay, slave; I must employ thee.
  As thou wilt win my favor, good my knave,
  Do one thing for me that I shall entreat.
COSTARD. When would you have it done, sir?
BEROWNE. O, this afternoon.   145
COSTARD. Well, I will do it, sir. Fare you well.
BEROWNE. O, thou knowest not what it is.
COSTARD. I shall know, sir, when I have done it.
BEROWNE. Why, villain, thou must know first.

---

122 *significant* i.e., letter   123 *ward* defense   127 *incony* darling
127 *Jew* (sense is unclear; perhaps a diminutive of "juvenal" or
"juvenile")   131 *inkle* a kind of linen tape   132 *carries it* it beats
everything   133 *French crown* a gold coin; with quibble on bald-
ness produced by the French disease, i.e., syphilis   133 *out of*
without using   135 *carnation* flesh colored

COSTARD. I will come to your worship to-morrow morn-
    ing.   150
BEROWNE. It must be done this afternoon. Hark, slave,
    it is but this:
    The princess comes to hunt here in the park,
    And in her train there is a gentle lady:
    When tongues speak sweetly, then they name her
        name,   155
    And Rosaline they call her. Ask for her,
    And to her white hand see thou do commend
    This sealed-up counsel. There's thy guerdon: go.
COSTARD. Gardon, O sweet gardon!* Better than remu-
    neration, eleven-pence farthing better. Most sweet   160
    gardon! I will do it, sir, in print. Gardon—remunera-
    tion.   *Exit.*
BEROWNE. O, and I, forsooth, in love!
    I, that have been love's whip,
    A very beadle to a humorous sigh,
    A critic, nay, a night-watch constable,   165
    A domineering pedant o'er the boy,
    Than whom no mortal so magnificent.
    This wimpled, whining, purblind, wayward boy,
    This signior junior, giant-dwarf, Dan Cupid,
    Regent of love-rimes, lord of folded arms,   170
    The anointed sovereign of sighs and groans,
    Liege of all loiterers and malcontents,
    Dread prince of plackets, king of codpieces,
    Sole imperator and great general
    Of trotting paritors—O my little heart!   175

158 *counsel* i.e., the letter   158 *guerdon* reward   161 *in print*
exactly   164 *beadle . . . sigh* a public whipper of a melancholy
sigh   166 *boy* i.e., Cupid   167 *magnificent* boastful(?)   arro-
gant(?)   168 *wimpled* muffled   168 *purblind* stone-blind   169
Dan don, i.e., master or sir   170 *folded arms* (a lover's pose)
173 *plackets* petticoats or slits in them, possibly with obscene
implication   173 *codpieces* flap or bag covering a man's crotch,
hence "man," often with obscene connotation   175 *paritors* officers of the bishop's court, among whose duties was discovering
cases of fornication

And I to be a corporal of his field,
And wear his colors like a tumbler's hoop!
What? I love, I sue, I seek a wife,
A woman that is like a German clock,
Still a-repairing, ever out of frame,   180
And never going aright, being a watch,
But being watched that it may still go right!
Nay, to be perjured, which is worst of all;
And, among three, to love the worst of all;
A whitely wanton with a velvet brow,   185
With two pitch balls stuck in her face for eyes.
Ay, and, by heaven, one that will do the deed,
Though Argus were her eunuch and her guard.
And I to sigh for her, to watch for her,
To pray for her! Go to, it is a plague   190
That Cupid will impose for my neglect
Of his almighty dreadful little might.
Well, I will love, write, sigh, pray, sue, groan:
Some men must love my lady, and some Joan.
[Exit.]

◀§ IV. i §▶

*Enter the Princess, a Forester, her Ladies [Maria,
Katharine, Rosaline], and her Lords [Boyet and
others].*

PRINCESS. Was that the king that spurred his horse so
    hard
Against the steep uprising of the hill?
BOYET. I know not, but I think it was not he.

176 *corporal* (a corporal held a higher position than he does now)
177 *tumbler's hoop* i.e., one decorated with vari-colored ribbons
185 *whitely* pale   187 *do the deed* i.e., the sexual act   188 *Argus*
the hundred-eyed guard, charged by Juno to keep Jupiter from making love to Io   194 *Joan* an ordinary woman or country wench
(proverbial)

PRINCESS. Whoe'er 'a was, 'a showed a mounting mind.
Well, lords, to-day we shall have our dispatch;   5
On Saturday we will return to France.
Then, forester, my friend, where is the bush
That we must stand and play the murderer in?
FORESTER. Hereby, upon the edge of yonder coppice,
A stand where you may make the fairest shoot.   10
PRINCESS. I thank my beauty, I am fair that shoot,
And thereupon thou speak'st the fairest shoot.
FORESTER. Pardon me, madam, for I meant not so.
PRINCESS. What, what? First praise me, and again say
no?
O short-lived pride! Not fair? Alack for woe!   15
FORESTER. Yes, madam, fair.
PRINCESS.   Nay, never paint me now:
Where fair is not, praise cannot mend the brow.
Here, good my glass, take this for telling true;
Fair payment for foul words is more than due.
FORESTER. Nothing but fair is that which you inherit.   20
PRINCESS. See, see, my beauty will be saved by merit.
O heresy in fair, fit for these days,
A giving hand, though foul, shall have fair praise.
But come, the bow. Now mercy goes to kill,
And shooting well is then accounted ill.   25
Thus will I save my credit in the shoot:
Not wounding, pity would not let me do 't;
If wounding, then it was to show my skill,
That more for praise than purpose meant to kill.
And out of question so it is sometimes,   30
Glory grows guilty of detested crimes,
When, for fame's sake, for praise, an outward part,
We bend to that the working of the heart;

IV.i.10 *stand* a concealed structure from which ladies of rank could
shoot at game with crossbows   16 *paint* flatter   18 *glass* mirror,
i.e., the forester   20 *inherit* possess   21 *merit* i.e., alms-giving
22 *in fair* to beauty   29 *than purpose* than useful or sporting purposes   30 *out of question* beyond doubt   31 *Glory* i.e., the thirst
for glory   33 *bend* i.e., add

As I for praise alone now seek to spill
The poor deer's blood, that my heart means no ill.   35
BOYET. Do not curst wives hold that self-sovereignty
Only for praise' sake, when they strive to be
Lords o'er their lords?
PRINCESS. Only for praise; and praise we may afford
To any lady that subdues a lord.   40

Enter [Costard, the] Clown.

BOYET. Here comes a member of the commonwealth.
COSTARD. God dig-you-den all. Pray you, which is the
head lady?
PRINCESS. Thou shalt know her, fellow, by the rest that
have no heads.   45
COSTARD. Which is the greatest lady, the highest?
PRINCESS. The thickest and the tallest.
COSTARD. The thickest and the tallest: it is so. Truth is
truth.
An your waist, mistress, were as slender as my wit,
One o' these maids' girdles for your waist should be
fit.   50
Are not you the chief woman? You are the thickest
here.
PRINCESS. What's your will, sir? What's your will?
COSTARD. I have a letter from Monsieur Berowne to one
Lady Rosaline.
PRINCESS. O thy letter, thy letter! He's a good friend of
mine.   55
Stand aside, good bearer. Boyet, you can carve;
Break up this capon.
BOYET.   I am bound to serve.
This letter is mistook; it importeth none here.
It is writ to Jaquenetta.
PRINCESS.   We will read it, I swear.
Break the neck of the wax, and every one give ear.   60
BOYET. [*reads*] "By heaven, that thou art fair is most in-

36 *curst* shrewish   42 *God dig-you-den* God give you good even-
(ing)   57 *capon* love-letter   58 *importeth* concerns

fallible; true that thou art beauteous; truth itself that
thou art lovely. More fairer than fair, beautiful than
beauteous, truer than truth itself, have commiseration
on thy heroical vassal. The magnanimous and most 65
illustrate king Cophetua set eye upon the pernicious
and indubitate beggar Zenelophon, and he it was that
might rightly say *veni, vidi, vici*; which to anathomize
in the vulgar, O base and obscure vulgar! *videlicet*, he
came, saw, and overcame.* (He came, one; saw, two; 70
overcame, three. Who came? The king. Why did he
come? To see. Why did he see? To overcome. To
whom came he? To the beggar. What saw he? The
beggar. Who overcame he? The beggar. The conclusion is victory. On whose side? The king's. The cap- 75
tive is enriched. On whose side? The beggar's. The
catastrophe is a nuptial. On whose side? The king's?
No, on both in one, or one in both. I am the king, for
so stands the comparison; thou the beggar, for so witnesseth thy lowliness.) Shall I command thy love? I 80
may. Shall I enforce thy love? I could. Shall I entreat
thy love? I will. (What shalt thou exchange for rags?
Robes. For tittles? Titles. For thyself? Me.) Thus, expecting thy reply, I profane my lips on thy foot, my
eyes on thy picture, and my heart on thy every part. 85

    Thine in the dearest design of industry,
                Don Adriano de Armado.*
Thus dost thou hear the Nemean lion roar
  'Gainst thee, thou lamb, that standest as his prey.
(Submissive fall his princely feet before,
  And he from forage will incline to play. 90
But if thou strive, poor soul, what art thou then?
Food for his rage, repasture for his den.")*

---

66 *illustrate* illustrious   67 *indubitate* unquestioned   67 *Zenelophon* Penelophon in the old ballad   68 *anathomize* old spelling
for "anatomize"(?) mock-Latin for "annotate"(?)   77 *catastrophe*
conclusion   83 *tittles* trifles   85 *industry* zealous courtship   87
Nemean lion (slain by Hercules)   90 *from forage . . . play* from
seeking food will turn to play   92 *repasture* food

PRINCESS. What plume of feathers is he that indited this
letter?

What vane? What weathercock? Did you ever hear
better?

(BOYET. I am much deceived but I remember the style.   95

PRINCESS. Else your memory is bad, going o'er it erewhile.) *

BOYET. This Armado is a Spaniard that keeps here in
court;

A phantasime, a Monarcho, and one that makes sport
To the prince and his book-mates.

PRINCESS.   Thou fellow, a word.
Who gave thee this letter?

COSTARD.   I told you, my lord.   100

PRINCESS. To whom shouldst thou give it?

COSTARD.   From my lord to my lady.

PRINCESS. From which lord, to which lady?

COSTARD. From my lord Berowne, a good master of mine,
To a lady of France, that he called Rosaline.

PRINCESS. Thou hast mistaken his letter. Come, lords,
away.   105

Here, sweet, put up this; 'twill be thine another day.
*Exeunt [Princess, Katharine, Forester,
and Attendants].*

BOYET. Who is the suitor? Who is the suitor?

ROSALINE.   Shall I teach you to know?

BOYET. Ay, my continent of beauty.

ROSALINE.   Why, she that bears the bow.
Finely put off!

BOYET. My lady goes to kill horns, but if thou marry,   110

---

95 *style* (pun on "stile")   96 *erewhile* even now   98 *phantasime*
fantastic fellow   98 *Monarcho* (an allusion to a fantastic Italian,
touched with megalomania, who frequented Elizabeth's court some
years before 1580)   105 *mistaken* taken to the wrong person   106
Here, sweet . . . day here, sweet (giving letter to Rosaline), put
this away; you will receive the one intended for you some other day
107 *suitor* (pronounced shooter)   109 *Finely put off* you're nicely
dismissed   110 *kill horns* shoot deer

Hang me by the neck if horns that year miscarry.
Finely put on!

ROSALINE. Well then, I am the shooter.

BOYET.   And who is your deer?

ROSALINE. If we choose by the horns, yourself. Come not
near.
Finely put on, indeed!

MARIA. You still wrangle with her, Boyet, and she strike
at the brow.

BOYET. But she herself is hit lower. Have I hit her now?

ROSALINE. Shall I come upon thee with an old saying
that was a man when King Pepin of France was a
little boy, as touching the hit it?

BOYET. So I may answer thee with one as old—that was
a woman when Queen Guinever of Britain was a little
wench, as touching the hit it.

ROSALINE. "Thou canst not hit it, hit it, hit it,
Thou canst not hit it, my good man.

BOYET.   "An I cannot, cannot, cannot,
An I cannot, another can."*

                    Exit [Rosaline].*

COSTARD. By my troth, most pleasant, how both did fit it!

MARIA. A mark marvellous well shot, for they both did
hit it.

BOYET. A mark! O mark but that mark: a mark, says my
lady!
Let the mark have a prick in 't, to mete at, if it may
be.

MARIA. Wide o' the bow hand! I' faith your hand is out.

COSTARD. Indeed 'a must shoot nearer, or he'll ne'er hit
the clout.

111-12 *if horns . . . put on* if a cuckold is not made that year.
That's nicely hit!   118 *come upon thee* strike back at thee   119
King Pepin father of Charlemagne, died 768   124-27 *Thou . . .
can* a song to a dance tune; both song and dance are mentioned in
Elizabethan literature; the tune is quoted in Chappell's *Popular
Music of the Olden Time* (1859)   129 *mark* target   131 *prick*
center of the target   131 *mete at* measure with the eye   132
Wide . . . hand wide of the mark   133 *clout* center pin of the
target, painted white

BOYET. An if my hand be out, then belike your hand is in.

COSTARD. Then will she get the upshoot by cleaving the
    pin.   135

MARIA. Come, come, you talk greasily; your lips grow
    foul.

COSTARD. She's too hard for you at pricks. Sir, challenge
    her to bowl.

BOYET. I fear too much rubbing. Good night, my good
    owl.   [*Exeunt Boyet and Maria.*]

COSTARD. By my soul, a swain, a most simple clown!
    Lord, lord, how the ladies and I have put him down!   140
    O' my troth, most sweet jests, most incony vulgar wit!
    When it comes so smoothly off, so obscenely as it
        were, so fit.
    Armado to th' one side; O, a most dainty man,
    To see him walk before a lady, and to bear her fan!
    To see him kiss his hand, and how most sweetly 'a
        will swear!   145
    And his page o' t'other side, that handful of wit,
    Ah, heavens, it is a most pathetical nit!
                                    Shout within.
    Sola, sola!   [*Exit.*]

135 *upshoot* best shot at any point of the contest   135 *cleaving the
pin* i.e., the clout   136 *greasily* indecently   137 *at pricks* unau-
thorized archery   138 *rubbing* (in bowling the technical term for
one bowl touching another)   141 *incony* darling   143–47 *Armado
. . . nit* (this description of Armado and Moth, unrelated to the previous
dialogue, indicates that either a portion of the scene was
omitted in printing the play or this scene was incompletely revised)
147 *pathetical nit* touching mite   148 *Sola, sola* (Costard's halloo
suggests a hunting cry)

ᴥᔥ IV. ii ᔥᴥ

Enter Dull, Holofernes the Pedant, and Nathaniel.

NATHANIEL. Very reverend sport, truly, and done in the
testimony of a good conscience.

HOLOFERNES. The deer was, as you know, *sanguis*, in
blood; ripe as the pomewater, who now hangeth like
a jewel in the ear of *coelo*, the sky, the welkin, the
heaven; and anon falleth like a crab on the face of
terra, the soil, the land, the earth.

NATHANIEL. Truly, Master Holofernes, the epithets are
sweetly varied, like a scholar at the least: but, sir, I
assure ye it was a buck of the first head.

HOLOFERNES. Sir Nathaniel, *haud credo*.*

DULL. 'Twas not a *haud credo*; 'twas a pricket.

HOLOFERNES. Most barbarous intimation! Yet a kind of
insinuation, as it were, *in via*, in way, of explication;
facere, as it were, replication, or rather, *ostentare*, to
show, as it were, his inclination—after his undressed,
unpolished, uneducated, unpruned, untrained, or,
rather, unlettered, or, ratherest, unconfirmed fashion
—to insert again my *haud credo* for a deer.

DULL. I said the deer was not a haud credo; 'twas a
pricket.

HOLOFERNES. Twice sod simplicity, *bis coctus!*
O thou monster Ignorance, how deformèd dost thou
look!

IV.ii.1–2 *in the testimony of a good conscience* with the approbation
of a godly conscience   3–4 *in blood* in perfect condition   4 *pomewater* a kind of apple   6 *crab* crab-apple   10 *of the first head*
with antlers, i.e., in its fifth year   11 *haud credo* I do not believe
it   12 *not . . . credo* (Dull mistakes "haud credo" for a type of
deer)   12 *pricket* a two-year old male deer   13 *intimation* inter-
ruption   14 *insinuation* insertion   21 *Twice sod . . . bis coctus*
twice sodden, i.e., boiled, simplicity (probably with reference to
twice-cooked colewort)

NATHANIEL.* Sir, he hath never fed of the dainties that
    are bred in a book.

He hath not eat paper, as it were; he hath not drunk
    ink.

His intellect is not replenished; he is only an animal,   25
    only sensible in the duller parts.

And such barren plants are set before us that we
    thankful should be,

Which we of taste and feeling are, for those parts that
    do fructify in us more than he;

For as it would ill become me to be vain, indiscreet,
    or a fool,

So were there a patch set on learning, to see him in a
    school.   30

But, *omne bene*, say I, being of an old father's mind,

Many can brook the weather that love not the wind.

DULL. You two are book-men. Can you tell me by your
    wit,

What was a month old at Cain's birth that's not five
    weeks old as yet?*

HOLOFERNES. *Dictynna*, goodman Dull. *Dictynna*, good-
    man Dull.   35

DULL. What is *Dictynna*?

NATHANIEL. A title to Phoebe, to Luna, to the moon.

HOLOFERNES. The moon was a month old when Adam
    was no more,

And raught not to five weeks when he came to five-
    score.

Th' allusion holds in the exchange.   40

DULL. 'Tis true indeed; the collusion holds in the ex-
    change.

HOLOFERNES. God comfort thy capacity! I say th' allu-
    sion holds in the exchange.

---

30 *patch* fool   31 *omne bene* all's well   31 *father's* wise man's
32 *brook* endure   35 *Dictynna* (an uncommon title for Diana, the
moon)   39 *raught* reached   40 *Th' allusion . . . exchange* the
jest (or riddle) is true even with the exchange of names, i.e., Adam
for Cain

DULL. And I say the pollution holds in the exchange, for the moon is never but a month old; and I say beside that 'twas a pricket that the princess killed. 45

HOLOFERNES. Sir Nathaniel, will you hear an extemporal epitaph on the death of the deer? And, to humor the ignorant, call I the deer the princess killed, a pricket.

NATHANIEL. *Perge*, good Master Holofernes, *perge*, so it 50 shall please you to abrogate scurrility.

HOLOFERNES. I will something affect the letter, for it argues facility.*

> The preyful princess pierced and pricked a pretty
>   pleasing pricket;
> Some say a sore, but not a sore, till now made sore
>   with shooting. 55
> The dogs did yell. Put el to sore, then sorel jumps
>   from thicket;
> Or pricket, sore, or else sorel, the people fall a hoot-
>   ing.
> If sore be sore, then el to sore makes fifty sores, O
>   sorel!
> Of one sore I an hundred make by adding but one
>   more L.

NATHANIEL. A rare talent! 60

DULL. If a talent be a claw, look how he claws him with a talent.

HOLOFERNES. This is a gift that I have, simple, simple; a foolish extravagant spirit, full of forms, figures, shapes, objects, ideas, apprehensions, motions, revolutions. 65 These are begot in the ventricle of memory, nourished in the womb of pia mater, and delivered upon the mellowing of occasion. But the gift is good in those in whom it is acute, and I am thankful for it.

---

50 *Perge* proceed   51 *abrogate scurrility* abolish indecency   52 *something affect the letter* somewhat assume the letter, i.e., the practice of alliteration   55 *sore* deer of the fourth year   56 *sorel* deer of the third year   59 *L* i.e., the Roman numeral for fifty   61 *talent* (pun on talon)   61 *claws* quibble on (1) scratches (2) flatters   66 *ventricle* one of the three sections of the brain, according to Vicary (1548)   67 *pia mater* the membrane enclosing the brain

NATHANIEL. Sir, I praise the Lord for you, and so may
my parishioners; for their sons are well tutored by
you, and their daughters profit very greatly under you.
You are a good member of the commonwealth.

HOLOFERNES. Mehercle, if their sons be ingenious, they
shall want no instruction; if their daughters be capable, I will put it to them. But, *vir sapit qui pauca
loquitur*. A soul feminine saluteth us.*

Enter Jaquenetta and [Costard,] the Clown.

JAQUENETTA. God give you good morrow, Master Parson.

HOLOFERNES. Master Parson, *quasi* pers-one? And if one
should be pierced, which is the one?

COSTARD. Marry, Master Schoolmaster, he that is likest
to a hogshead.*

HOLOFERNES. Of piercing a hogshead! a good lustre of
conceit in a turf of earth, fire enough for a flint, pearl
enough for a swine: 'tis pretty, it is well.

JAQUENETTA. Good Master Parson, be so good as read
me this letter.* It was given me by Costard, and sent
me from Don Armado. I beseech you read it.

HOLOFERNES. *Fauste, precor gelida quando pecus omne
sub umbra ruminat*, and so forth. Ah, good old Mantuan. I may speak of thee as the traveller doth of
Venice:

> *Venetia, Venetia,*
> *Chi non ti vede, non ti pretia.*

74 *Mehercle* by Hercules!   75–76 *capable* i.e., (1)intellectually (2)
sexually   76–77 *vir . . . loquitur* "That Man is wise that speaketh
few things or words"; so translated in Lyly's *Grammar*   78 *Parson*
(pronounced "person")   79 *quasi* that is   80 *pierced* ("pierce"
pronounced as "purse"; "piercing a hogshead" may have been slang
for "getting drunk")   82 *hogshead* dull-witted person   83–84
lustre of conceit gleam of wit   89–90 *Fauste . . . ruminat* "Faus-
tus, I pray while all the cattle ruminate beneath the cool shade";
from the first eclogue of Mantuanus, a piece widely taught in the
schools of Shakespeare's day   92–93 *Venetia . . . pretia* "Venice,
Venice, who seeth thee not, praiseth thee not"

Old Mantuan, old Mantuan! Who understandeth
thee not, loves thee not. *Ut, re, sol, la, mi, fa.* Under   9
pardon, sir, what are the contents? or, rather, as
Horace says in his—What my soul! verses?

NATHANIEL. Ay, sir, and very learned.

HOLOFERNES. Let me hear a staff, a stanze, a verse. *Lege,
domine.*   100

NATHANIEL. [*reads*] "If love make me forsworn, how
shall I swear to love?
　　Ah, never faith could hold if not to beauty vowed!
Though to myself forsworn, to thee I'll faithful prove;
　　Those thoughts to me were oaks, to thee like osiers
　　　bowed.
Study his bias leaves and makes his book thine
　　eyes,   105
　　Where all those pleasures live that art would com-
　　　prehend.
If knowledge be the mark, to know thee shall suffice:
　　Well learnèd is that tongue that well can thee com-
　　　mend,
All ignorant that soul that sees thee without wonder;
　　Which is to me some praise, that I thy parts admire.   110
Thy eye Jove's lightning bears, thy voice his dreadful
　　thunder,
　　Which, not to anger bent, is music and sweet fire.
Celestial as thou art, O pardon love this wrong,
That sings heaven's praise with such an earthly
　　tongue!"

HOLOFERNES. You find not the apostrophus, and so miss   115
the accent. Let me supervise the canzonet. Here are
only numbers ratified; but, for the elegancy, facility,

---

95 *Ut* . . . *fa* (an incorrect rendering of the gamut or musical
scale; "do" has since replaced "ut")   99–100 *Lege, domine* read,
master   104 *thoughts* thoughts which   105 *Study . . . eyes* schol-
arship forsakes its disposition and makes your eyes its books   115
find not pay no attention to   115 *apostrophus* apostrophe, i.e.,
contractions (?) caesura (J. D. Wilson) (?)   116 *canzonet* brief
song   117 *numbers ratified* verses in correct meter

and golden cadence of poesy, caret. Ovidius Naso was
the man; and why indeed "Naso" but for smelling out
the odoriferous flowers of fancy, the jerks of inven-   120
tion? *Imitari* is nothing. So doth the hound his master, the ape his keeper, the tired horse his rider. But
damosella virgin, was this directed to you?

JAQUENETTA. Ay, sir, from one Monsieur Berowne, one
of the strange queen's lords.   125

HOLOFERNES. I will overglance the superscript. "To the
snow-white hand of the most beauteous Lady Rosaline." I will look again on the intellect of the letter,
for the nomination of the party writing to the person
written unto. "Your ladyship's, in all desired employ-   130
ment, Berowne." Sir Nathaniel, this Berowne is one
of the votaries with the king; and here he hath framed
a letter to a sequent of the stranger queen's, which accidentally, or by the way of progression, hath miscar-
ried. Trip and go, my sweet; deliver this paper into   135
the royal hand of the king; it may concern much.
Stay not thy compliment; I forgive thy duty. Adieu.

JAQUENETTA. Good Costard, go with me. Sir, God save
your life.

COSTARD. Have with thee, my girl.   140

Exit [with Jaquenetta].

NATHANIEL. Sir, you have done this in the fear of God
very religiously; and, as a certain father saith—

HOLOFERNES. Sir, tell not me of the father; (I do fear
colorable colors.) But to return to the verses—did
they please you, Sir Nathanial?   145

NATHANIEL. Marvellous well for the pen.

HOLOFERNES. I do dine to-day at the father's of a certain

---

118 *caret* it is missing   118 *Ovidius Naso* Publius Ovidius Naso, or
Ovid, the Latin poet; Naso from "nasus," nose   121 *Imitari* to
imitate   126 *superscript* address   128 *intellect of the letter* mind
who was responsible for the letter(?) signature(?)   133 *sequent*
follower   135 *Trip and go* a morris dance   137 *Stay . . . compliment* do not stand on ceremony   137 *duty* curtsy   144 *colorable colors* plausible pretexts   146 *pen* style(?) penmanship(?)

pupil of mine, where, if before repast it shall please you to gratify the table with a grace, I will, on my privilege I have with the parents of the aforesaid child or pupil, undertake your *ben venuto;* where I will prove those verses to be very unlearned, neither savoring of poetry, wit, nor invention. I beseech your society.

NATHANIEL. And thank you too: for society, saith the text, is the happiness of life.

HOLOFERNES. And, certes, the text most infallibly concludes it. [*to Dull*]* Sir, I do invite you too; you shall not say me nay: *pauca verba*. Away! The gentles are at their game, and we will to our recreation. *Exeunt.*

ᦰᔩ I V . iii ᦖᕽ

*Enter Berowne with a paper in his hand, alone.**

BEROWNE. The king he is hunting the deer; I am coursing myself. They have pitched a toil; I am toiling in a pitch, pitch that defiles. Defile—a foul word! Well, set thee down, sorrow; for so they say the fool said, and so say I, and I the fool. Well proved, wit! By the Lord, this love is as mad as Ajax: it kills sheep; it kills me—I a sheep. Well proved again o' my side! I will not love; if I do, hang me. I' faith, I will not. O but her eye! By this light, but for her eye, I would not love her—yes, for her two eyes. Well, I do nothing in the world but lie, and lie in my throat. By heaven, I do love, and it hath taught me to rime, and to be melancholy; and here is part of my rime, and here my melancholy. Well, she hath one o' my sonnets already.

151 *ben venuto* welcome   158 *pauca verba* few words   IV.iii.2 *pitched a toil* set a snare   4 *set . . . sorrow* (see I.i.297 for same expression)   6 *Ajax* a Greek hero; angered at not being awarded Achilles' arms, he went mad and in frenzy slew sheep which he believed were the Greek leaders

The clown bore it, the fool sent it, and the lady hath   15
it: sweet clown, sweeter fool, sweetest lady! By the
world, I would not care a pin if the other three were
in. Here comes one with a paper: God give him grace
to groan!   *He stands aside.*

The King ent'reth [with a paper].

KING. Ay me!
BEROWNE. Shot, by heaven! Proceed, sweet Cupid; thou
   hast thumped him with thy bird-bolt under the left   20
   pap. In faith, secrets!
KING. [*reads*] "So sweet a kiss the golden sun gives not
      To those fresh morning drops upon the rose,
   As thy eye-beams when their fresh rays have smote
      The night of dew that on my cheeks down flows.   25
   Nor shines the silver moon one half so bright
      Through the transparent bosom of the deep
   As doth thy face, through tears of mine, give light.
      Thou shin'st in every tear that I do weep;
   (No drop but as a coach doth carry thee;   30
      So ridest thou triumphing in my woe.
   Do but behold the tears that swell in me,
      And they thy glory through my grief will show;) *
   But do not love thyself—then thou will keep
   My tears for glasses and still make me weep.   35
   O queen of queens, how far dost thou excel
   No thought can think, nor tongue of mortal tell!"
How shall she know my griefs? I'll drop the paper.
Sweet leaves, shade folly. Who is he comes here?

*Enter Longaville [with a paper]. The King steps
   aside.*

What, Longaville? and reading? Listen, ear.   40
BEROWNE. Now, in thy likeness, one more fool appear!
LONGAVILLE. Ay me! I am forsworn.

---

18 *in* i.e., in love   20 *bird-bolt* blunt arrow for shooting birds
21 *pap* breast, i.e., heart   35 *glasses* mirrors

BEROWNE. Why, he comes in like a perjure, wearing
    papers.

KING. In love, I hope: sweet fellowship in shame!

BEROWNE. One drunkard loves another of the name.   45

LONGAVILLE. Am I the first that have been perjured so?

BEROWNE. I could put thee in comfort, not by two that
    I know.
    Thou mak'st the triumviry, (the corner-cap of society,
    The shape of love's Tyburn,) that hangs up sim-
        plicity.*

LONGAVILLE. I fear these stubborn lines lack power to
    move.   50
    O sweet Maria, empress of my love!
    These numbers will I tear, and write in prose.

BEROWNE. O, rimes are guards on wanton Cupid's hose;
    Disfigure not his shop.

LONGAVILLE.   This same shall go.

                                    He reads the sonnet.

"Did not the heavenly rhetoric of thine eye,   55
    'Gainst whom the world cannot hold argument,
Persuade my heart to this false perjury?
    Vows for thee broke deserve not punishment.
A woman I forswore, but I will prove,
    Thou being a goddess, I forswore not thee.   60
My vow was earthly, thou a heavenly love;
    (Thy grace being gained, cures all disgrace in me.
Vows are but breath, and breath a vapor is:
    Then thou, fair sun, which on my earth dost shine,
Exhal'st this vapor-vow; in thee it is.   65
    If broken then, it is no fault of mine;)*
If by me broke, what fool is not so wise
To lose an oath to win a paradise?"

43 *perjure* perjurer   43 *wearing papers* i.e., as signs announcing
his offense   48 *triumviry* trio   48 *corner-cap* (allusion to a priest's
or judge's cap, and possibly to triangular shape sometimes used for
the Tyburn gallows)   53 *guards* trimmings   54 *shop* i.e., codpiece
62 *grace* favor   65 *Exhal'st* draws in

BEROWNE. This is the liver-vein, which makes flesh a deity,

A green goose a goddess. Pure, pure idolatry.   70

God amend us, God amend! We are much out o' the way.

Enter Dumaine [with a paper].

LONGAVILLE. By whom shall I send this?—Company? Stay.   [*He steps aside.*]

BEROWNE. All hid, all hid—an old infant play.

Like a demi-god here sit I in the sky,

And wretched fools' secrets heedfully o'er-eye.   75

More sacks to the mill! O heavens, I have my wish!

Dumaine transformed: four woodcocks in a dish!

DUMAINE. O most divine Kate!

BEROWNE. O most profane coxcomb!

DUMAINE. By heaven, the wonder in a mortal eye!   80

BEROWNE. By earth, she is not, corporal; there you lie.

DUMAINE. Her amber hairs for foul have amber quoted.

BEROWNE. An amber-colored raven was well noted.

DUMAINE. As upright as the cedar.

BEROWNE.   Stoop, I say;

Her shoulder is with child.

DUMAINE.   As fair as day.   85

BEROWNE. Ay, as some days, but then no sun must shine.

DUMAINE. O that I had my wish!

LONGAVILLE.   And I had mine!

KING. And I mine too, good Lord!

BEROWNE. Amen, so I had mine. Is not that a good word?

DUMAINE. I would forget her, but a fever she   90

Reigns in my blood, and will rememb'red be.

69 *liver-vein* i.e., way to express passion (the liver was considered the center of passion) . 70 *green goose* (see I.i.97)   71 *out o' the way* astray   76 *More . . . mill* more work to be done (proverbial)   77 *woodcocks* i.e., fools   81 *corporal* (see III.i.176)   82 *Her amber . . . quoted* her amber hairs by example have shown real amber to be foul   83 *raven* (1) fowl (2) foul, as contrasted with fair amber   84 *Stoop* stooped, bent   85 *with child* has a hump

BEROWNE. A fever in your blood? Why, then incision
  Would let her out in saucers. Sweet misprision!
DUMAINE. Once more I'll read the ode that I have writ.
BEROWNE. Once more I'll mark how love can vary wit.   95
  Dumaine reads his sonnet.
DUMAINE. "On a day—alack the day!—
  Love, whose month is ever May,
  Spied a blossom passing fair
  Playing in the wanton air.
  Through the velvet leaves the wind,   100
  All unseen, can passage find;
  That the lover, sick to death,
  Wished himself the heaven's breath.
  Air, quoth he, thy cheeks may blow;
  Air, would I might triumph so!   105
  But, alack, my hand is sworn
  Ne'er to pluck thee from thy thorn.
  (Vow, alack, for youth unmeet,
  Youth so apt to pluck a sweet!)
  Do not call it sin in me,   110
  That I am forsworn for thee;
  Thou for whom Jove would swear
  Juno but an Ethiop were;
  And deny himself for Jove,
  Turning mortal for thy love."   115
This will I send, and something else more plain,
That shall express my true love's fasting pain.
O would the King, Berowne, and Longaville
Were lovers too! Ill, to example ill,
Would from my forehead wipe a perjured note: 120
For none offend, where all alike do dote.
LONGAVILLE. [*steps forth*] Dumaine, thy love is far from
    charity,
  That in love's grief desir'st society.
  You may look pale, but I should blush, I know,
  To be o'erheard and taken napping so.   125

93 *let her out in saucers* let the blood out into saucers (commonly
used for bloodletting)   93 *misprision* mistake   117 *fasting* hun-
gry   120 *note* sign

KING. [*steps forth*] Come, sir, you blush! As his your
　　case is such;
　　You chide at him, offending twice as much.
　　You do not love Maria! Longaville
　　Did never sonnet for her sake compile,
　　Nor never lay his wreathèd arms athwart   130
　　His loving bosom to keep down his heart.
　　I have been closely shrouded in this bush,
　　And marked you both, and for you both did blush.
　　I heard your guilty rimes, observed your fashion,
　　Saw sighs reek from you, noted well your passion.   135
　　Ay me! says one; O Jove! the other cries;
　　One, her hairs were gold; crystal, the other's eyes.
　　[*To Longaville*] You would for paradise break faith
　　　and troth;
　　[*To Dumaine*] And Jove, for your love, would infringe
　　　an oath.
　　What will Berowne say when that he shall hear   140
　　Faith infringèd, which such zeal did swear?
　　How will he scorn! How will he spend his wit!
　　How will he triumph, leap and laugh at it!
　　For all the wealth that ever I did see,
　　I would not have him know so much by me.   145
BEROWNE. [*steps forth*] Now step I forth to whip hypoc-
　　risy.
　　Ah, good my liege, I pray thee pardon me.
　　Good heart, what grace hast thou, thus to reprove
　　These worms for loving, that art most in love?
　　Your eyes do make no coaches; in your tears   150
　　There is no certain princess that appears;
　　You'll not be perjured, 'tis a hateful thing.
　　Tush, none but minstrels like of sonneting!
　　But are you not ashamed? Nay, are you not,
　　All three of you, to be thus much o'ershot?   155

130 *lay his . . . athwart* (the stance of a lover)   135 *reek* steam
145 *by* concerning   150 *coaches* (Berowne mocks the King's poetry; see IV.iii.30)   155 *o'ershot* wide of your mark, hence gone
astray

You found his mote; the king your mote did see;
But I a beam to find in each of three.
O what a scene of fool'ry have I seen,
Of sighs, of groans, of sorrow, and of teen!
O me, with what strict patience have I sat,   160
To see a king transformèd to a gnat;
To see great Hercules whipping a gig,
And profound Solomon to tune a jig,
And Nestor play at push-pin with the boys,
And critic Timon laugh at idle toys!   165
Where lies thy grief? O, tell me, good Dumaine.
And gentle Longaville, where lies thy pain?
And where my liege's? All about the breast.
A caudle, ho!
KING.   Too bitter is thy jest.
Are we betrayed thus to thy over-view?   170
BEROWNE. Not you by me, but I betrayed to you.
I that am honest, I that hold it sin
To break the vow I am engagèd in,
I am betrayed by keeping company
With men like you, men of inconstancy.   175
When shall you see me write a thing in rime?
Or groan for Joan? or spend a minute's time
In pruning me? When shall you hear that I
Will praise a hand, a foot, a face, an eye,
A gait, a state, a brow, a breast, a waist,   180
A leg, a limb—
KING.   Soft! Whither away so fast?
A true man or a thief, that gallops so?
BEROWNE. I post from love. Good lover, let me go.

159 *teen* grief   161 *gnat* i.e., to insignificance   162 *gig* top, spun
by whipping   163 *jig* (term applies to the dance and the music for
the dance)   164 *Nestor* the Greek leader renowned for age and
wisdom   164 *push-pin* (a game usually played by children)   165
critic over-critical   165 *Timon* (famed for his misanthropy)   165
laugh at delight in   169 *caudle* thin beverage usually administered
to the sick   178 *pruning* preening, such as trimming one's beard
180 *state* stance or posture   180 *brow* countenance   183 *post*
ride away, flee

Enter Jaquenetta and [Costard, the] Clown.

JAQUENETTA. God bless the king!

KING.   What present has thou there?

COSTARD. Some certain treason.

KING.   What makes treason here?   185

COSTARD. Nay, it makes nothing, sir.

KING.   If it mar nothing neither,
The treason and you go in peace away together.

JAQUENETTA. I beseech your Grace let this letter be read:
Our parson misdoubts it; 'twas treason, he said.

KING. Berowne, read it over.   190

                    He [Berowne] reads the letter.
Where hadst thou it?

JAQUENETTA. Of Costard.

KING. Where hadst thou it?

COSTARD. Of Dun Adramadio, Dun Adramadio.

                    [*Berowne tears the letter.*]

KING. How now, what is in you? Why dost thou tear it?   195

BEROWNE. A toy, my liege, a toy. Your Grace needs not
fear it.

LONGAVILLE. It did move him to passion, and therefore
let's hear it.

DUMAINE. [*picking up the pieces*] It is Berowne's writing,
and here is his name.

BEROWNE. [*to Costard*] Ah, you whoreson loggerhead,
you were born to do me shame.

Guilty, my lord, guilty. I confess, I confess.   200

KING. What?

BEROWNE. That you three fools lacked me fool to make
up the mess.

He, he, and you: and you my liege, and I,
Are pick-purses in love, and we deserve to die.

O dismiss this audience, and I shall tell you more.   205

DUMAINE. Now the number is even.

---

189 *misdoubts* suspects   196 *toy* trifle   199 *loggerhead* blockhead
202 *mess* a party of four at table, as was usual at feasts

BEROWNE.   True, true; we are four.
  Will these turtles be gone?
KING.   Hence, sirs, away.
COSTARD. Walk aside the true folk, and let the traitors
    stay.   [*Exeunt Costard and Jaquenetta.*]
BEROWNE. Sweet lords, sweet lovers, O, let us embrace!
  As true we are as flesh and blood can be;   210
  The sea will ebb and flow, heaven show his face:
  Young blood doth not obey an old decree.
  We cannot cross the cause why we were born;
  Therefore, of all hands must we be forsworn.
KING. What, did these rent lines show some love of
    thine?   215
BEROWNE. Did they? quoth you. Who sees the heavenly
    Rosaline,
  That, like a rude and savage man of Inde,
  At the first opening of the gorgeous east,
  Bows not his vassal head and, strooken blind,
  Kisses the base ground with obedient breast?   220
  What peremptory eagle-sighted eye
  Dares look upon the heaven of her brow,
  That is not blinded by her majesty?
KING. What zeal, what fury, hath inspired thee now?
  My love, her mistress, is a gracious moon;   225
  She, an attending star, scarce seen a light.
BEROWNE. My eyes are then no eyes, nor I Berowne.
  O, but for my love, day would turn to night!
  Of all complexions the culled sovereignty
  Do meet, as at a fair, in her fair cheek,   230
  Where several worthies make one dignity,
  Where nothing wants that want itself doth seek.
  Lend me the flourish of all gentle tongues—
  Fire, painted rhetoric! O, she needs it not.

207 *turtles* turtledoves   213 *cross* oppose   214 *of all hands* on all
sides, i.e., wherever we turn   215 *rent* torn   217 *Inde* India   221
peremptory bold   229 *the culled sovereignty* those selected as best
232 *wants* is lacking   234 *painted* artificial

To things of sale a seller's praise belongs;   235
She passes praise; then praise too short doth blot.
A withered hermit, five-score winters worn,
Might shake off fifty, looking in her eye:
Beauty doth varnish age as if new-born,
And gives the crutch the cradle's infancy.   240
O, 'tis the sun that maketh all things shine!
KING. By heaven, thy love is black as ebony.
BEROWNE. Is ebony like her? O wood divine!
  A wife of such wood were felicity.
  O, who can give an oath? Where is a book?   245
  That I may swear beauty doth beauty lack,
  If that she learn not of her eye to look.
  No face is fair that is not full so black.
KING. O paradox! Black is the badge of hell,
  The hue of dungeons, and the school of night;   250
  And beauty's crest becomes the heavens well.
BEROWNE. Devils soonest tempt, resembling spirits of
    light.
  O, if in black my lady's brows be decked,
  It mourns that painting and usurping hair
  Should ravish doters with a false aspect;   255
  And therefore is she born to make black fair.
  Her favor turns the fashion of the days,
  For native blood is counted painting now;
  And therefore red that would avoid dispraise
  Paints itself black to imitate her brow.   260
DUMAINE. To look like her are chimney-sweepers black.
LONGAVILLE. And since her time are colliers counted
    bright.
KING. And Ethiops of their sweet complexion crack.
DUMAINE. Dark needs no candles now, for dark is light.

247 *she learn . . . to look* beauty does not learn with Rosaline's
eyes to see   250 *school* (allusion to supposed "school" or coterie
of liberal thinkers, such as Raleigh, Chapman, Harriot, etc.)   251
crest badge   254 *usurping* false   257 *favor turns* face changes
258 *native blood* natural complexion   263 *crack* brag

BEROWNE. Your mistresses dare never come in rain,   265
  For fear their colors should be washed away.
KING. 'Twere good yours did; for, sir, to tell you plain,
  I'll find a fairer face not washed to-day.
BEROWNE. I'll prove her fair, or talk till doomsday here.
KING. No devil will fright thee then so much as she.   270
DUMAINE. I never knew man hold vile stuff so dear.
LONGAVILLE. Look, here's thy love—[Shows his shoe.]
  my foot and her face see.
BEROWNE. O, if the streets were pavèd with thine eyes,
  Her feet were much too dainty for such tread.
DUMAINE. O vile! Then, as she goes, what upward lies   275
  The street should see as she walked overhead.
KING. But what of this? Are we not all in love?
BEROWNE. O, nothing so sure, and thereby all forsworn.
KING. Then leave this chat; and, good Berowne, now
    prove
  Our loving lawful and our faith not torn.   280
DUMAINE. Ay, marry, there; some flattery for this evil.
LONGAVILLE. O some authority how to proceed;
  Some tricks, some quillets, how to cheat the devil.
DUMAINE. Some salve for perjury.
BEROWNE.   O, 'tis more than need.
  Have at you, then, affection's men-at-arms!*   285
  Consider what you first did swear unto:
  To fast, to study, and to see no woman:
  Flat treason 'gainst the kingly state of youth.
  Say, can you fast? Your stomachs are too young,
  And abstinence engenders maladies.   290
  And where that you have vowed to study, lords,
  In that each of you have forsworn his book.
  Can you still dream and pore and thereon look?
  For when would you, my lord, or you, or you,
  Have found the ground of study's excellence   295

270 *then* i.e., at doomsday   283 *quillets* quibbles   285 *affection's
men-at-arms* love's soldiers   291 *where that* in the fact that   292
In that in that very vow   292 *book* i.e., his true text, a woman's
face   295 *ground* basis

Without the beauty of a woman's face?
From women's eyes this doctrine I derive:
They are the ground, the books, the academes,
From whence doth spring the true Promethean fire.
Why, universal plodding poisons up   300
The nimble spirits in the arteries,
As motion and long-during action tires
The sinewy vigor of the traveller.
Now, for not looking on a woman's face,
You have in that forsworn the use of eyes,   305
And study too, the causer of your vow;
For where is any author in the world
Teaches such beauty as a woman's eye?
Learning is but an adjunct to ourself,
And where we are our learning likewise is.   310
Then when ourselves we see in ladies' eyes,
Do we not likewise see our learning there?
O, we have made a vow to study, lords,
And in that vow we have forsworn our books;
For when would you, my liege, or you, or you,   315
In leaden contemplation have found out
Such fiery numbers as the prompting eyes
Of beauty's tutors have enriched you with?
Other slow arts entirely keep the brain,
And therefore, finding barren practisers,   320
Scarce show a harvest of their heavy toil;
But love, first learnèd in a lady's eyes,
Lives not alone immurèd in the brain,
But, with the motion of all elements,
Courses as swift as thought in every power,   325
And gives to every power a double power,
Above their functions and their offices.*
It adds a precious seeing to the eye:
A lover's eyes will gaze an eagle blind.
A lover's ear will hear the lowest sound,   330

299 *Promethean fire* spark of originality; from Prometheus who
stole fire from the gods and gave it to man   317 *fiery numbers*
passionate verses

When the suspicious head of theft is stopped.
Love's feeling is more soft and sensible
Than are the tender horns of cockled snails.
Love's tongue proves dainty Bacchus gross in taste.
For valor, is not Love a Hercules,   335
Still climbing trees in the Hesperides?
Subtle as Sphinx; as sweet and musical
As bright Apollo's lute, strung with his hair.
And when Love speaks, the voice of all the gods
Make heaven drowsy with the harmony.   340
Never durst poet touch a pen to write
Until his ink were temp'red with Love's sighs:
O, then his lines would ravish savage ears
And plant in tyrants mild humility.
From women's eyes this doctrine I derive.   345
They sparkle still the right Promethean fire;
They are the books, the arts, the academes,
That show, contain, and nourish all the world;
Else none at all in aught proves excellent.
Then fools you were these women to forswear,*   350
Or, keeping what is sworn, you will prove fools.
For wisdom's sake, a word that all men love,
Or for love's sake, a word that loves all men,
Or for men's sake, the authors of these women,
Or women's sake, by whom we men are men,   355
Let us once lose our oaths to find ourselves,
Or else we lose ourselves to keep our oaths.
It is religion to be thus forsworn,
For charity itself fulfils the law
And who can sever love from charity?   360

KING. Saint Cupid then! And, soldiers, to the field!
BEROWNE. Advance your standards, and upon them,
    lords!

---

331 *suspicious head of theft* acute watchfulness of the thief   332
sensible sensitive   333 *cockled snails* snails in shells   336 *Hesperides* garden of the golden apples   353 *loves* is pleasing to(?)

Pell-mell, down with them! But be first advised,
In conflict that you get the sun of them.

LONGAVILLE. Now to plain-dealing; lay these glozes by: 365
Shall we resolve to woo these girls of France?

KING. And win them too; therefore let us devise
Some entertainment for them in their tents.

BEROWNE. First from the park let us conduct them
thither;
Then homeward every man attach the hand   370
Of his fair mistress. In the afternoon
We will with some strange pastime solace them,
Such as the shortness of the time can shape;
For revels, dances, masks, and merry hours
Forerun fair Love, strewing her way with flowers.*   375

KING. Away, away! No time shall be omitted
That will be time, and may by us be fitted.

BEROWNE. Allons! allons! Sowed cockle reaped no corn;
And justice always whirls in equal measure.
Light wenches may prove plagues to men forsworn;   380
If so, our copper buys no better treasure.*   [Exeunt.]

꙳ V. i ꙳

*Enter [Holofernes,] the Pedant, [Nathaniel,] the
Curate, and Dull, [the Constable].*

HOLOFERNES. *Satis quid sufficit.*

NATHANIEL. I praise God for you, sir. Your reasons at
dinner have been sharp and sententious: pleasant
without scurrility, witty without affection, audacious
without impudency, learned without opinion, and   5

364 *the sun of* the advantage of, i.e., by having one's back to the
sun   365 *glozes* purposeless words, pretenses   378 *cockle . . . corn*
a weed easily mistaken for "corn," i.e., wheat   380 *men forsworn*
men who have broken their oaths   381 *copper* coin   V.i.1 *Satis
quid sufficit* Anglicized as "enough is as good as a feast"   2 *reasons*
discourse   4 *affection* affectation   5 *opinion* self-conceit, arrogance

strange without heresy. I did converse this quondam
day with a companion of the king's, who is entitled,
nominated, or called, Don Adriano de Armado.

HOLOFERNES. *Novi hominem tanquam te.* His humor is
lofty, his discourse peremptory, his tongue filed, his   10
eye ambitious, his gait majestical, and his general behavior vain, ridiculous, and thrasonical. He is too
picked, too spruce, too affected, too odd, as it were,
too peregrinate, as I may call it.

NATHANIEL. A most singular and choice epithet.   15
                    *Draw out his table-book.**

HOLOFERNES. He draweth out the thread of his verbosity
finer than the staple of his argument. I abhor such
fanatical phantasimes, such insociable and point-
devise companions; such rackers of orthography as to
speak "dout" fine when he should say "doubt"; "det"   20
when he should pronounce "debt"—d, e, b, t, not
d, e, t. He clepeth a calf "cauf"; half "hauf"; neighbor
vocatur "nebor," neigh abbreviated "ne." This is
abhominable, which he would call "abominable." It
insinuateth me of insanie. *Ne intelligis, domine?* To   25
make frantic, lunatic.

NATHANIEL. *Laus Deo bone intelligo.*

HOLOFERNES. *Bone? Bone* for *bene!* Priscian a little
scratched*—'twill serve.

*Enter [Armado, the] Braggart, [Moth, the] Boy,
[and Costard, the Clown].*

6 *strange* original   9 *Novi . . . te* I know the man as well as I
know you   10 *filed* polished   12 *thrasonical* boastful   12–13 *too
picked, too spruce* too fastidious, too overelegant   13 *peregrinate*
i.e., foreign in fashion and manner   15s.d. *table-book* notebook
17 *staple* fiber (of wool)   18 *fanatical* extravagant   18 *phantasimes* (see IV.i.98)   18–19 *point-devise* precise, exact   20 *fine* i.e.,
with nicety   22 *clepeth* calls   23 *vocatur* is called   25 *insinuateth me of insanie* suggests madness to me(?) makes me frantic(?)
25 *Ne . . . domine* do you understand, master parson   26 *Laus
. . . intelligo* praise God, good sir, I understand   27 *Priscian* a
Latin grammarian, widely read in the Middle Ages

NATHANIEL. *Videsne quis venit?*

HOLOFERNES. *Video, et gaudeo.*   30

ARMADO. [*to Moth*] Chirrah!

HOLOFERNES. *Quare* "chirrah," not "sirrah"?*

ARMADO. Men of peace, well encountered.

HOLOFERNES. Most military sir, salutation.

MOTH. [*aside to Cosard*] They have been at a great feast   35
of languages and stolen the scraps.

COSTARD. O, they have lived long on the alms-basket of
words. I marvel thy master hath not eaten thee for a
word; for thou art not so long by the head as honorificabilitudinitatibus. Thou art easier swallowed than a   40
flapdragon.

MOTH. Peace! The peal begins.

ARMADO. Monsieur, are you not lett'red?

MOTH. Yes, yes, he teaches boys the horn-book. What is
a, b, spelled backward with the horn on his head?   45

HOLOFERNES. Ba, *pueritia*, with a horn added.

MOTH. Ba, most silly sheep with a horn. You hear his
learning.

HOLOFERNES. *Quis, quis*, thou consonant?*

MOTH. The last of the five vowels, if you repeat them; or   50
the fifth, if I.

HOLOFERNES. I will repeat them: a, e, i—

MOTH. The sheep. The other two concludes it—o, u.

ARMADO. Now, by the salt wave of the Mediterranean, a
sweet touch, a quick venew of wit! Snip, snap, quick   55
and home! It rejoiceth my intellect. True wit!

MOTH. Offered by a child to an old man—which is wit-
old.

29 *Videsne quis venit* do you see who comes   30 *Video, et gaudeo*
I see and rejoice   32 *Quare* why   37 *alms-basket* basket or tub
into which left-overs were collected for distribution to the poor
39–40 *honorificabilitudinitatibus* (supposedly the longest word
known)   41 *flapdragon* a plum or raisin set afire in liquor and
swallowed flaming as part of a game   42 *peal* mighty sound   44
horn-book a primer for teaching the alphabet   46 *pueritia* child
49 *Quis* who   49 *consonant* nonentity   55 *venew* bout, specifically
in fencing   57 *wit-old* (quibble on "wittol," i.e., contented cuckold)

HOLOFERNES. What is the figure? What is the figure?

MOTH. Horns.

HOLOFERNES. Thou disputes like an infant. Go whip thy   60
gig.

MOTH. Lend me your horn to make one, and I will whip
about your infamy *manu cita*. A gig of a cuckold's
horn.

COSTARD. An I had but one penny in the world, thou
shouldst have it to buy gingerbread. (Hold, there is
the very remuneration I had of thy master,) thou half-   65
penny purse of wit, thou pigeon-egg of discretion. (O,
an the heavens were so pleased that thou wert but my
bastard, what a joyful father wouldest thou make
me!) * Go to, thou hast it *ad dunghill*, at the fingers'
ends, as they say.

HOLOFERNES. O, I smell false Latin! *"Dunghill"* for   70
unguem.

ARMADO. *Arts-man, preambulate.* We will be singled
from the barbarous. Do you not educate youth at the
charge-house on the top of the mountain?

HOLOFERNES. Or *mons*, the hill.

ARMADO. At your sweet pleasure, for the mountain.   75

HOLOFERNES. I do, *sans question*.

ARMADO. Sir, it is the king's most sweet pleasure and
affection to congratulate the princess at her pavilion
in the *posteriors* of this day, which the rude multitude
call the afternoon.   80

HOLOFERNES. The *posterior* of the day, most generous
sir, is liable, congruent, and measurable for the afternoon. The word is well culled, chose, sweet and apt,
I do assure you, sir, I do assure.

ARMADO.* Sir, the king is a noble gentleman, and my   85

---

58 *figure* i.e., of speech   60 *gig* top   62 *manu cita* with ready hand
65–66 *halfpenny purse* small purse for holding a single coin   69 *ad
dunghill* (Costard's error for "ad unguem," to the fingernail or finger's end)   71 *Arts-man* scholar   71 *preambulate* "after you"   71
singled separated   73 *charge-house* school   82 *liable* apt   83
chose choice

familiar, I do assure ye, very good friend. For what is
inward between us, let it pass. I do beseech thee remember thy courtesy. I beseech thee apparel thy head.
And among other importunate and most serious de-
signs, and of great import indeed, too—but let that   90
pass; for I must tell thee, it will please his Grace, by
the world, sometime to lean upon my poor shoulder,
and with his royal finger thus dally with my excrement,
with my mustachio—but, sweet heart, let that pass.
By the world, I recount no fable: some certain special   95
honors it pleaseth his greatness to impart to Armado,
a soldier, a man of travel, that hath seen the world—
but let that pass. The very all of all is: but, sweet
heart, I do implore secrecy, that the king would have
me present the princess, sweet chuck, with some de-   100
lightful ostentation, or show, or pageant, or antic, or
fire-work. Now, understanding that the curate and
your sweet self are good at such eruptions and sudden
breaking out of mirth, as it were, I have acquainted
you withal, to the end to crave your assistance.

HOLOFERNES. Sir, you shall present before her the Nine   105
Worthies. Sir Nathaniel, as concerning some entertainment of time, some show in the posterior of this
day, to be ren'dred by our assistance, the king's command, and this most gallant, illustrate, and learned
gentleman, before the princess: I say, none so fit as to   110
present the Nine Worthies.

NATHANIEL. Where will you find men worthy enough to
present them?

---

87 *inward* confidential   87–88 *remember . . . head* (apparently
Holofernes has removed his hat which Armado takes to be a mark
of courtesy, whether or not intended so by Holofernes)   93 *excrement* an outgrowth of the body, such as hair   101 *antic* a grotesque pageant   105–6 *Nine Worthies* three pagans: Hector,
Alexander, Julius Caesar; three Jews: Joshua, David, Judas Maccabaeus; three Christians: King Arthur, Charlemagne, Sir Guy of
Warwick or Godfrey of Bouillon. Traditionally Hercules and Pompey were not included among the Worthies

HOLOFERNES. Joshua, yourself; myself; and this gallant
gentleman, Judas Maccabaeus; this swain, because of   115
his great limb or joint, shall pass Pompey the Great;
the page, Hercules—

ARMADO. Pardon, sir, error. He is not quantity enough
for that Worthy's thumb; he is not so big as the end
of his club.   120

HOLOFERNES. Shall I have audience? He shall present
Hercules in minority. His enter and exit shall be
strangling a snake; and I will have an apology for that
purpose.

MOTH. An excellent device! So if any of the audience
hiss, you may cry, "Well done, Hercules! Now thou   125
crushest the snake!" That is the way to make an
offense gracious, though few have the grace to do it.

ARMADO. For the rest of the Worthies?

HOLOFERNES. I will play three myself.

MOTH. Thrice-worthy gentleman!   130

ARMADO. Shall I tell you a thing?*

HOLOFERNES. We attend.

ARMADO. We will have, if this fadge not, an antic. I
beseech you, follow.

HOLOFERNES. *Via*, goodman Dull!* Thou hast spoken no   135
word all this while.

DULL. Nor understood none neither, sir.

HOLOFERNES. Allons! we will employ thee.

DULL. I'll make one in a dance, or so; or I will play on
the tabor to the Worthies, and let them dance the hay. 140

HOLOFERNES. Most dull, honest Dull. To our sport,
away!   *Exeunt.*

114–17 *Joshua . . . Hercules* (Holofernes' assignment of roles does
not conform to later pageant; some scholars cite the discrepancy
as evidence of revision)   116 *pass* surpass(?) pass for, i.e., repre-
sent(?)   121 *have audience* be heard   121–23 *He shall . . . snake*
(as an infant Hercules strangled two snakes in his cradle)   123
apology explanation   133 *fadge not* doesn't turn out well   133
antic (see V.i.101)   135 *Via* away! (an exclamation of encourage-
ment)   140 *tabor* small drum   140 *the hay* a country dance similar to a reel

✑ V . ii ✑

Enter the Ladies [Princess, Katharine, Rosaline, and Maria].

PRINCESS. Sweet hearts, we shall be rich ere we depart
If fairings come thus plentifully in.
A lady walled about with diamonds!*
Look you what I have from the loving king.
ROSALINE. Madam, came nothing else along with that?   5
PRINCESS. Nothing but this? yes, as much love in rime
As would be crammed up in a sheet of paper,
Writ o' both sides the leaf, margent and all,
That he was fain to seal on Cupid's name.*
ROSALINE. That was the way to make his godhead wax,   10
For he hath been five thousand year a boy.
KATHARINE. Ay, and a shrewd unhappy gallows too.
ROSALINE. You'll ne'er be friends with him: 'a killed your
sister.
KATHARINE. He made her melancholy, sad, and heavy;*
And so she died. Had she been light, like you,   15
Of such a merry, nimble, stirring spirit,
She might ha' been a grandam ere she died;
And so may you, for a light heart lives long.
ROSALINE. What's your dark meaning, mouse, of this
light word?
KATHARINE. A light condition in a beauty dark.   20
ROSALINE. We need more light to find your meaning out.
KATHARINE. You'll mar the light by taking it in snuff;
Therefore, I'll darkly end the argument.

V.ii.2 *fairings* items purchased at a fair   3 A *lady . . . diamonds*
(the design of the gift)   8 *margent* margin   10 *wax* increase   12
shrewd unhappy gallows cunning misery-making fellow who deserves
hanging(?)   15–26 *light* (quibbles upon the various senses of light,
i.e., frivolous, merry, insignificant, wanton, light in weight)   22 *in
snuff* (1) in anger (2) in disgust, at odor of a snuffed candle

ROSALINE. Look, what you do, you do it still i' th' dark.

KATHARINE. So do not you, for you are a light wench.   25

ROSALINE. Indeed I weigh not you, and therefore light.

KATHARINE. You weigh me not? O! that's you care not
    for me.

ROSALINE. Great reason; for past cure is still past care.

PRINCESS. Well bandied both, a set of wit well played.

    But, Rosaline, you have a favor too: 30

    Who sent it? and what is it?

ROSALINE.   I would you knew.

    An if my face were but as fair as yours,

    My favor were as great. Be witness this.

    Nay, I have verses too, I thank Berowne:

    The numbers true; and, were the numb'ring too,   35

    I were the fairest goddess on the ground.

    I am compared to twenty thousand fairs.

    O, he hath drawn my picture in his letter!

PRINCESS. Anything like?

ROSALINE. Much in the letters, nothing in the praise.   40

PRINCESS. Beauteous as ink: a good conclusion.

KATHARINE. Fair as a text B in a copy-book.*

ROSALINE. 'Ware pencils, ho! Let me not die your
    debtor,

    My red dominical,* (my golden letter.

    O, that your face were not so full of O's!   4

---

26 *I weigh not you* I do not weigh as much as you   28 *past cure*
without remedy   28 *past care* without concern   29 *bandied* hit
back and forth (a tennis term)   30, 33 *favor* present; with pun on
appearance   35 *numbers* cadence   35 *numb'ring too* i.e., number-
ing of my qualities also true   37 *fairs* beauties   40 *Much in . . .
praise* very similar in the darkness of the written letter, not at all
similar in the subject of the praise   42 *a text B* (here B represents
blackness, either because its inscription in text or formal writing is
particularly black or because it is the first letter of the word
"black")   43 *'Ware pencils* beware pencils, i.e., brushes for stip-
ling   44 *red dominical* red letter to denote Sundays in old alma-
nacs; golden letter refers either to the letter itself or to its background; thus Rosaline glances at Katharine's ruddiness (pock
marks?) and amber hair   45 *O's* spots, marks

PRINCESS. A pox of that jest, and I beshrew all shrows!)*
  But, Katharine, what was sent to you from fair Du-
    maine?
KATHARINE. Madam, this glove.
PRINCESS.   Did he not send you twain?
KATHARINE. Yes, madam; and moreover,
  Some thousand verses of a faithful lover: 50
  A huge translation of hypocrisy,
  Vilely compiled, profound simplicity.
MARIA. This, and these pearls, to me sent Longaville.
  The letter is too long by half a mile.*
PRINCESS. I think no less. Dost thou not wish in heart 55
  The chain were longer and the letter short?
MARIA. Ay, or I would these hands might never part.
PRINCESS. We are wise girls to mock our lovers so.
ROSALINE. They are worse fools to purchase mocking so.
  That same Berowne I'll torture ere I go.   60
  O that I knew he were but in by th' week!
  How I would make him fawn, and beg, and seek,
  And wait the season, and observe the times,
  And spend his prodigal wits in bootless rimes,
  And shape his service wholly to my hests,   65
  And make him proud to make me proud that jests!
  So Pair-Taunt like would I o'ersway his state
  That he should be my fool, and I his fate.
PRINCESS. None are so surely caught, when they are
    catched,
  As wit turned fool. (Folly, in wisdom hatched,   70
  Hath wisdom's warrant and the help of school
  And wit's own grace to grace a learnèd fool.)*
ROSALINE. The blood of youth burns not with such excess
  As gravity's revolt to wantonness.
MARIA. Folly in fools bears not so strong a note   75

46 *beshrew* curse 46 *shrows* shrews 59 *so* i.e., by means of
love letters and gifts 61 *in by th' week* firmly ensnared 65 *hests*
i.e., behests, commands 66 *to make me proud* i.e., of him 67
Pair-Taunt (the winning hand in an obsolete card-game called Post
and Pair)

As fool'ry in the wise when wit doth dote;
Since all the power thereof it doth apply
To prove, by wit, worth in simplicity.*

Enter Boyet.

PRINCESS. Here comes Boyet, and mirth is in his face.
BOYET. O, I am stabbed with laughter! Where's her   80
     Grace?
PRINCESS. Thy news, Boyet?
BOYET.   Prepare, madam, prepare!
     Arm, wenches, arm! Encounters mounted are
     Against your peace. Love doth approach disguised,
     Armèd in arguments; you'll be surprised.
     Muster your wits, stand in your own defense,   85
     Or hide your heads like cowards, and fly hence.
PRINCESS. Saint Denis to Saint Cupid! What are they
     That charge their breath against us? Say, scout, say.
BOYET. Under the cool shade of a sycamore
     I thought to close mine eyes some half an hour,   90
     When, lo, to interrupt my purposed rest,
     Toward that shade I might behold addrest
     The king and his companions! Warily
     I stole into a neighbor thicket by,
     And overheard what you shall overhear: 95
     That, by and by, disguised they will be here.
     Their herald is a pretty knavish page,
     That well by heart hath conned his embassage.
     Action and accent did they teach him there:
     "Thus must thou speak, and thus thy body bear."   100
     And ever and anon they made a doubt
     Presence majestical would put him out;
     "For," quoth the king, "an angel shalt thou see;
     Yet fear not thou, but speak audaciously."

78 *simplicity* folly   84 *surprised* taken unawares   87 *Saint Denis*
(the Princess opposes her patron, the patron saint of France, to
the patron saint of the approaching lovers)   92 *addrest* headed
directly   98 *conned* learned   101–2 *made a doubt . . . him out*
indicated concern that the princely presence would make him forget
his lines

The boy replied, "An angel is not evil;   105
I should have feared her had she been a devil."
With that all laughed and clapped him on the shoul-
    der,
Making the bold wag by their praises bolder.
One rubbed his elbow thus, and fleered, and swore
A better speech was never spoke before.   110
Another, with his finger and his thumb,
Cried "Via, we will do 't, come what will come!"
The third he capered and cried, "All goes well!"
The fourth turned on the toe, and down he fell.
With that they all did tumble on the ground   115
With such a zealous laughter, so profound,
That in this spleen ridiculous appears,
To check their folly, passion's solemn tears.
PRINCESS. But what, but what? Come they to visit us?
BOYET. They do, they do; and are apparelled thus,   120
    Like Muscovites or Russians, as I guess.
    Their purpose is to parle, to court and dance;
    And every one his love-feat will advance
    Unto his several mistress, which they'll know
    By favors several which they did bestow.   125
PRINCESS. And will they so? The gallants shall be tasked:
    For, ladies, we will every one be masked,*
    And not a man of them shall have the grace,
    Despite of suit, to see a lady's face.
    Hold, Rosaline, this favor thou shalt wear,   130
    And then the king will court thee for his dear:
    Hold, take thou this, my sweet, and give me thine;
    So shall Berowne take me for Rosaline.
    And change you favors too; so shall your loves
    Woo contrary, deceived by these removes.   135

---

109 *One rubbed his elbow* (a gesture of satisfaction and delight)
109 *fleered* grinned   111 *with . . . thumb* i.e., snapping them in
high spirits   112 *Via* (see V.i.135)   117 *spleen ridiculous* ridiculous fit of laughter   122 *parle* confer   123 *love-feat* effort at
courtship   126 *tasked* tested   129 *suit* entreaty   135 *removes*
gifts removed from one to another

ROSALINE. Come on, then, wear the favors most in sight.
KATHARINE. But in this changing what is your intent?
PRINCESS. The effect of my intent is to cross theirs.
    They do it but in mockery merriment,
    And mock for mock is only my intent.
    Their several counsels they unbosom shall
    To loves mistook and so be mocked withal
    Upon the next occasion that we meet,
    With visages displayed, to talk and greet.
ROSALINE. But shall we dance if they desire us to 't?
PRINCESS. No, to the death we will not move a foot,
    Nor to their penned speech render we no grace,
    But while 'tis spoke each turn away her face.
BOYET. Why, that contempt will kill the speaker's heart,
    And quite divorce his memory from his part.
PRINCESS. Therefore I do it, and I make no doubt
    The rest will ne'er come in, if he be out.
    There's no such sport as sport by sport o'erthrown,
    To make theirs ours, and ours none but our own.
    So shall we stay, mocking intended game,
    And they, well mocked, depart away with shame.
                                    Sound Trumpets.
BOYET. The trumpet sounds. Be masked. The maskers
    come.

        *Enter Blackamoors with music; [Moth,] the Boy,
            with a speech, and the rest of the Lords dis-
            guised.**

MOTH. "All hail, the richest beauties on the earth!"
BOYET. Beauties no richer than rich taffeta.
MOTH. "A holy parcel of the fairest dames,
                The Ladies turn their backs to him.
    That ever turned their—backs—to mortal views!"

---

136 *most in sight* conspicuously   139 *mockery merriment* merry
mockery, i.e., of the ladies   141 *several counsels* individual secrets
155 *intended game* the planned sport of the men(?)   159 *taffeta*
i.e., of their masks

BEROWNE. "Their eyes," villain, "their eyes."
MOTH. "That ever turned their eyes to mortal views!
　Out—"
BOYET. True. "Out" indeed.   165
MOTH. "Out of your favors, heavenly spirits, vouchsafe
　Not to behold"—
EROWNE. "Once to behold," rogue.
OTH. "Once to behold with your sun-beamèd eyes,
　—with your sun-beamèd eyes"—   170
YET. They will not answer to that epithet.
　You were best call it "daughter-beamèd eyes."
OTH. They do not mark me, and that brings me out.
ROWNE. Is this your perfectness? Be gone, you rogue!
　　　　　　　　　　　　　　　　　　[Exit Moth.]
OSALINE. What would these strangers? Know their
　minds, Boyet.   175
　If they do speak our language, 'tis our will
　That some plain man recount their purposes.
　Know what they would.
BOYET. What would you with the Princess?
BEROWNE. Nothing but peace and gentle visitation.*   180
ROSALINE. What would they, say they?
BOYET. Nothing but peace and gentle visitation.
ROSALINE. Why, that they have, and bid them so be
　gone.
BOYET. She says you have it and you may be gone.
KING. Say to her, we have measured many miles,   185
　To tread a measure with her on this grass.
BOYET. They say that they have measured many a mile,
　To tread a measure with you on this grass.
ROSALINE. It is not so. Ask them how many inches
　Is in one mile. If they have measured many,   190
　The measure then of one is easily told.
BOYET. If to come hither you have measured miles,
　And many miles, the princess bids you tell
　How many inches doth fill up one mile.*

165, 173 Out i.e., out of his part, having forgotten his speech   186
measure stately dance

BEROWNE. Tell her we measure them by weary steps.

BOYET. She hears herself.

ROSALINE.   How many weary steps,
Of many weary miles you have o'ergone,
Are numb'red in the travel of one mile?

BEROWNE. We number nothing that we spend for you.
Our duty is so rich, so infinite,
That we may do it still without account.
Vouchsafe to show the sunshine of your face,
That we, like savages, may worship it.

ROSALINE. My face is but a moon, and clouded too.

KING. Blessèd are clouds, to do as such clouds do.
Vouchsafe, bright moon, and these thy stars, to shine,
Those clouds removed, upon our watery eyne.

ROSALINE. O vain petitioner, beg a greater matter.
Thou now requests but moonshine in the water.

KING. Then in our measure do but vouchsafe one change.
Thou bid'st me beg; this begging is not strange.

ROSALINE. Play music then.* Nay, you must do it soon.
Not yet? no dance! thus change I like the moon.

KING. Will you not dance? How come you thus es-
trangèd?

ROSALINE. You took the moon at full, but now she's
changèd.

KING. Yet still she is the moon, and I the man.
The music plays; vouchsafe some motion to it.

ROSALINE. Our ears vouchsafe it.

KING.   But your legs should do it.

ROSALINE. Since you are strangers and come here by
chance,
We'll not be nice: take hands—we will not dance.

---

203 *like savages* (the Russians were so regarded by the Elizabeth-
ans)   204–5, 207 *clouded, clouds* (refers to masks worn by the
ladies)   207 *eyne* eyes   210 *change* round in dancing (Rosaline
takes it up as 'a change of the moon' line 213)   220 *nice* coy

KING. Why take we hands then?

ROSALINE.   Only to part friends.
Curtsy, sweet hearts; and so the measure ends.

KING. More measure of this measure! Be not nice.

ROSALINE. We can afford no more at such a price.

KING. Price you yourselves. What buys your company?   225

ROSALINE. Your absence only.

KING   That can never be.

ROSALINE. Then cannot we be bought: and so adieu,
Twice to your visor, and half once to you.

KING. If you deny to dance, let's hold more chat.

ROSALINE. In private then.

KING.   I am best pleased with that.   230
                    [*They converse apart.*]

BEROWNE. White-handed mistress, one sweet word with
thee.

PRINCESS. Honey, and milk, and sugar: there is three.

BEROWNE. Nay then, two treys, an if you grow so nice,
Metheglin, wort, and malmsey; well run, dice!
There's half a dozen sweets.

PRINCESS.   Seventh sweet, adieu.   235
Since you can cog, I'll play no more with you.

BEROWNE. One word in secret.

PRINCESS.   Let it not be sweet.

BEROWNE. Thou grievest my gall.

PRINCESS.   Gall! Bitter.

BEROWNE.   Therefore meet.
                    [*They converse apart.*]

DUMAINE. Will you vouchsafe with me to change a
word?

MARIA. Name it.

DUMAINE.   Fair lady—

220–223 *take hands . . . this measure* (the sequence of steps
leading to a dance were taking hands, curtsying, and kissing)   233
two treys i.e., I'll give my three for your three (a dicing term)
233 *nice* artful   234 *Metheglin* a Welsh beverage of honey,
water, and herbs   234 *wort* unfermented beer   234 *malmsey* a
strong sweet wine   236 *cog* cheat   238 *meet* fitting

MARIA.   Say you so? Fair lord—
Take that for your "fair lady."
DUMAINE.   Please it you,
As much in private, and I'll bid adieu.
                       [*They converse apart.*]
KATHARINE. What, was your vizard made without a
    tongue?
LONGAVILLE. I know the reason, lady, why you ask.
KATHARINE. O for your reason! Quickly, sir; I long.
LONGAVILLE. You have a double tongue within your mask
And would afford my speechless vizard half.
KATHARINE. "Veal," quoth the Dutchman. Is not "veal"
    a calf?
LONGAVILLE. A calf, fair lady?
KATHARINE.   No, a fair lord calf.
LONGAVILLE. Let's part the word.
KATHARINE.   No, I'll not be your half:
Take all and wean it; it may prove an ox.*
(LONGAVILLE. Look how you butt yourself in these sharp
    mocks.
Will you give horns, chaste lady? Do not so.
KATHARINE. Then die a calf before your horns do grow.
LONGAVILLE. One word in private with you ere I die.
KATHARINE. Bleat softly then. The butcher hears you
    cry.)   [*They converse apart.*]
BOYET. The tongues of mocking wenches are as keen
As is the razor's edge invisible,
Cutting a smaller hair than may be seen;
Above the sense of sense, so sensible
Seemeth their conference, their conceits have wings
Fleeter than arrows, bullets, wind, thought, swifter
    things.

---

243 *vizard* mask (visor)   248 V*eal* viel or "well" in German; with
triple pun: (1)on vizard or "veil" (2)on calf or "veal" (3)on
Longa*ville*   250 *your half* i.e., better half   253 *give horns* prove
unfaithful in marriage   260 *sensible* highly charged   261 *conceits*
images

ROSALINE. Not one word more, my maids! Break off,
    break off.

BEROWNE. By heaven, all dry-beaten with pure scoff!

KING. Farewell, mad wenches. You have simple wits.   265
                    Exeunt [King and Lords].

PRINCESS. Twenty adieus, my frozen Muscovits.
    Are these the breed of wits so wondered at?

BOYET. Tapers they are, with your sweet breaths puffed
    out.

ROSALINE. Well-liking wits they have; gross, gross; fat,
    fat.

PRINCESS. O poverty, in wit, kingly-poor flout!   270
    Will they not, think you, hang themselves to-night?
    Or ever but in vizards show their faces?
    This pert Berowne was out of count'nance quite.

ROSALINE. They were all in lamentable cases.
    The king was weeping-ripe for a good word.   275

PRINCESS. Berowne did swear himself out of all suit.

MARIA. Dumaine was at my service, and his sword:
    "No point," quoth I; (my servant straight was mute.)

KATHARINE. Lord Longaville said I came o'er his heart;
    (And trow you what he called me?)

PRINCESS   Qualm, perhaps.   280

KATHARINE. Yes, in good faith.

PRINCESS.   Go, sickness as thou art!

ROSALINE. Well, better wits have worn plain statute-
    caps.) *
    But will you hear? The king is my love sworn.

PRINCESS. And quick Berowne hath plighted faith to me.

KATHARINE. And Longaville was for my service born.   285

---

264 *dry-beaten* bruised by blows which do not draw blood   269
Well-liking plump   270 *kingly-poor flout* impoverished gibe; with
quibble on Rosaline's "well-li-king" wits   275 *weeping-ripe* on the
verge of tears   276 *out of all suit* without restraint(?) out of all
future courtship(?)   278 *No point* not at all   280 *trow you*
would you believe   280 *Qualm* spasm of illness, such as nausea
282 *plain statute-caps* unadorned caps which ordinary citizens were
required to wear

MARIA. Dumaine is mine as sure as bark on tree.

BOYET. Madam, and pretty mistresses, give ear.
    Immediately they will again be here
    In their own shapes, for it can never be
    They will digest this harsh indignity.

PRINCESS. Will they return?

BOYET.   They will, they will, God knows,
    And leap for joy though they are lame with blows.
    Therefore change favors, and when they repair,
    Blow like sweet roses in this summer air.

PRINCESS. How blow? how blow? Speak to be under-
    stood.

BOYET. Fair ladies, masked, are roses in their bud;
    Dismasked, their damask sweet commixture shown,
    Are angels vailing clouds, or roses blown.

PRINCESS. Avaunt, perplexity! What shall we do
    If they return in their own shapes to woo?

ROSALINE. Good madam, if by me you'll be advised,
    Let's mock them still, as well known as disguised.
    Let us complain to them what fools were here,
    Disguised like Muscovites in shapeless gear;
    And wonder what they were, and to what end
    Their shallow shows and prologue vilely penned,
    And their rough carriage so ridiculous,
    Should be presented at our tent to us.

BOYET. Ladies, withdraw. The gallants are at hand.

PRINCESS. Whip to your tents, as roes run o'er the land.
                        [Exeunt Princess and Ladies].

    Enter the King and the rest [Berowne, Dumaine,
        and Longaville].

KING. Fair sir, God save you. Where's the Princess?

BOYET. Gone to her tent. Please it your Majesty
    Command me any service to her thither?

---

293 *change favors* i.e., exchange or take back the gifts you first received   293 *repair* return   297 *damask sweet commixture shown*
the sweet mingling of their red and white complexion revealed   298
vailing dropping, lowering   299 *Avaunt* away, begone (directed at
Boyet)   304 *gear* dress

KING. That she vouchsafe me audience for one word.
BOYET. I will; and so will she, I know, my lord.   *Exit.*   315
BĒROWNE. This fellow pecks up wit, as pigeons pease,
  And utters it again when God doth please.
  He is wit's pedlar, and retails his wares
  At wakes and wassails, meetings, markets, fairs;
  And we that sell by gross, the Lord doth know,   320
  Have not the grace to grace it with such show.
  This gallant pins the wenches on his sleeve.
  Had he been Adam, he had tempted Eve.
  'A can carve too, and lisp. Why, this is he
  That kissed his hand away in courtesy.   325
  This is the ape of form, monsieur the nice,
  That, when he plays at tables, chides the dice
  In honorable terms. (Nay, he can sing
  A mean most meanly; and in ushering
  Mend him who can.)* The ladies call him sweet.   330
  The stairs, as he treads on them, kiss his feet.
  This is the flow'r that smiles on every one,
  To show his teeth as white as whalës-bone;
  And consciences that will not die in debt
  Pay him the due of "honey-tongued Boyet."   335
KING. A blister on his sweet tongue, with my heart,
  That put Armado's page out of his part!

  Enter the Ladies [with Boyet].

BEROWNE. See where it comes! Behavior, what wert thou,
  Till this madman showed thee? and what art thou
    now?*
KING. All hail, sweet madam, and fair time of day.   340
PRINCESS. "Fair" in "all hail" is foul, as I conceive.
KING. Construe my speeches better, if you may.

---

317 *utters* offers to sell   319 *wakes* all-night festivities   319 *was-sails* festivities marked by drinking   320 *by gross* wholesale   324 *carve* flatter(?) exhibit great affability(?)   326 *ape of form* mimic of fashion   327 *tables* backgammon   329 *mean* vocal part of middle range   329–30 *in ushering . . . can* in running before others, as a gentleman-in-waiting, beat him who can   338 *Behavior* good manners   339 *madman* madcap, jester

PRINCESS. Then wish me better; I will give you leave.
KING. We came to visit you, and purpose now
　　To lead you to our court. Vouchsafe it then.
PRINCESS. This field shall hold me, and so hold your vow.
　　Nor God nor I delights in perjured men.
KING. Rebuke me not for that which you provoke.
　　The virtue of your eye must break my oath.
PRINCESS. You nickname virtue. "Vice" you should have
　　　spoke;
　　For virtue's office never breaks men's troth.
　　Now, by my maiden honor, yet as pure
　　As the unsullied lily, I protest,
　　A world of torments though I should endure,
　　I would not yield to be your house's guest,
　　So much I hate a breaking cause to be
　　Of heavenly oaths, vowed with integrity.
KING. O, you have lived in desolation here,
　　Unseen, unvisited, much to our shame.
PRINCESS. Not so, my lord. It is not so, I swear.
　　We have had pastimes here and pleasant game.
　　A mess of Russians left us but of late.
KING. How, madam? Russians?
PRINCESS.　　　　　　　　　　Ay, in truth, my lord;
　　Trim gallants, full of courtship and of state.
ROSALINE. Madam, speak true. It is not so, my lord.
　　My lady, to the manner of the days,
　　In courtesy gives undeserving praise.
　　We four indeed confronted were with four
　　In Russian habit. Here they stayed an hour
　　And talked apace; and in that hour, my lord,
　　They did not bless us with one happy word.
　　I dare not call them fools; but this I think,
　　When they are thirsty, fools would fain have drink.
BEROWNE. This jest is dry to me. Gentle sweet,

346 *hold your vow* keep your oath unbroken   349 *virtue* (signifies
both goodness and power)   350 *nickname* name mistakingly   356
breaking disrupting   362 *mess* a party of four (see IV.iii.202)   366
to the manner of the days in the fashion of the times

Your wit makes wise things foolish. When we greet   375
With eyes best seeing heaven's fiery eye,
By light we lose light. Your capacity
Is of that nature that to your huge store
Wise things seem foolish and rich things but poor.

ROSALINE. This proves you wise and rich, for in my eye—   380

BEROWNE. I am a fool and full of poverty.

ROSALINE. But that you take what doth to you belong,
It were a fault to snatch words from my tongue.

BEROWNE. O, I am yours, and all that I possess.

ROSALINE. All the fool mine?

BEROWNE.   I cannot give you less.   385

ROSALINE. Which of the vizards was it that you wore?

BEROWNE. Where? when? what vizard? Why demand
you this?

ROSALINE. There, then, that vizard; that superfluous case
That hid the worse, and showed the better face.

KING. We were descried. They'll mock us now down-
right.   390

DUMAINE. Let us confess, and turn it to a jest.

PRINCESS. Amazed, my lord? Why looks your Highness
sad?

ROSALINE. Help! Hold his brows! He'll sound. Why look
you pale?
Seasick, I think, coming from Muscovy.

BEROWNE. Thus pour the stars down plagues for perjury.   395
Can any face of brass hold longer out?
Here stand I, lady; dart thy skill at me.
Bruise me with scorn, confound me with a flout,
Thrust thy sharp wit quite through my ignorance,
Cut me to pieces with thy keen conceit;   400
And I will wish thee never more to dance,
Nor never more in Russian habit wait.
O, never will I trust to speeches penned,

375 *foolish* seem foolish by comparison   375–77 W*hen . . . lose
light* when we look with the keenest eyesight at the sun, by its bril-
liance we lose our sight   393 *sound* swoon   398 *flout* sarcastic
comment   400 *conceit* imagination   402 *wait* i.e., as a servant

Nor to the motion of a schoolboy's tongue,
Nor never come in vizard to my friend,   405
Nor woo in rime, like a blind harper's song.
Taffeta phrases, silken terms precise,
Three-piled hyperboles, spruce affection,
Figures pedantical; these summer flies
Have blown me full of maggot ostentation.   410
I do forswear them; and I here protest
By this white glove (how white the hand, God knows)
Henceforth my wooing mind shall be expressed
In russet yeas and honest kersey noes.
And to begin: Wench—so God help me, law!—   415
My love to thee is sound, *sans* crack or flaw.
ROSALINE. *Sans* "*sans*," I pray you.
BEROWNE.   Yet I have a trick
Of the old rage. Bear with me, I am sick.
I'll leave it by degrees. Soft, let us see—
Write "Lord have mercy on us" on those three.   420
They are infected, in their hearts it lies;
They have the plague, and caught it of your eyes.
These lords are visited; you are not free,
For the Lord's tokens on you do I see.
PRINCESS. No, they are free that gave these tokens to us. 425
BEROWNE. Our states are forfeit, seek not to undo us.
ROSALINE. It is not so, for how can this be true,
That you stand forfeit, being those that sue?

---

405 *friend* sweetheart   408 *Three-piled hyperboles* extravagant exaggeration; three-piled velvet was the thickest and most expensive
velvet   408 *spruce affection* foppish affectation   409 *Figures* i.e.,
of speech   410 *blown* filled, by laying eggs as flies do in a carcass
414 *russet* cloth worn by peasants   414 *kersey* coarse woolen cloth
415 *law* la(?)   417 *sans* "*sans*" without affected words   420 *Lord
. . . us* (a plague warning posted on a house or appended to a
corpse to signify the presence of infection)   423 *visited* i.e., by the
plague   423 *free* i.e., of the infection   424 *tokens* plague-spots;
here Berowne is indicating the gifts previously sent to the ladies
425 *free* (1)of infection (2)generous   426 *Our . . . us* our prop-
erty is confiscated, do not try to undo the forfeiture of ourselves to
you   428 *sue* (1)plead (2)bring suit against us

BEROWNE. Peace! for I will not have to do with you.
ROSALINE. Nor shall not, if I do as I intend.   430
BEROWNE. Speak for yourselves; my wit is at an end.
KING. Teach us, sweet madam, for our rude transgression
    Some fair excuse.
PRINCESS.   The fairest is confession.
    Were you not here but even now disguised?
KING. Madam, I was.
PRINCESS.   And were you well advised?   435
KING. I was, fair madam.
PRINCESS.   When you then were here,
    What did you whisper in your lady's ear?
KING. That more than all the world I did respect her.
PRINCESS. When she shall challenge this, you will reject
    her.
KING. Upon mine honor, no.
PRINCESS.   Peace, peace, forbear!   440
    Your oath once broke, you force not to forswear.
KING. Despise me when I break this oath of mine.
PRINCESS. I will, and therefore keep it. Rosaline,
    What did the Russian whisper in your ear?
ROSALINE. Madam, he swore that he did hold me dear   445
    As precious eyesight, and did value me
    Above this world; adding thereto, moreover,
    That he would wed me, or else die my lover.
PRINCESS. God give thee joy of him. The noble lord
    Most honorably doth uphold his word.   450
KING. What mean you, madam? By my life, my troth,
    I never swore this lady such an oath.
ROSALINE. By heaven you did, and to confirm it plain
    You gave me this: but take it, sir, again.
KING. My faith and this the Princess I did give.   455
    I knew her by this jewel on her sleeve.
PRINCESS. Pardon me, sir, this jewel did she wear,

---

435 *well advised* in full possession of your senses   441 *Your oath
. . . forswear* having once broken your oath, you do not care if you
forswear, i.e., again

And Lord Berowne, I thank him, is my dear.
What, will you have me, or your pearl again?
BEROWNE. Neither of either: I remit both twain.   460
I see the trick on 't. Here was a consent,
Knowing aforehand of our merriment,
To dash it like a Christmas comedy.
Some carry-tale, some please-man, some slight zany,
Some mumble-news, some trencher-knight, some Dick   465
That smiles his cheek in years, and knows the trick
To make my lady laugh when she's disposed,
Told our intents before; which once disclosed,
The ladies did change favors, and then we,
Following the signs, wooed but the sign of she.   470
Now, to our perjury to add more terror,
We are again forsworn, in will and error.
Much upon this 'tis. [to Boyet] And might not you
Forestall our sport, to make us thus untrue?
Do not you know my lady's foot by th' squier,   475
And laugh upon the apple of her eye?
And stand between her back, sir, and the fire,
Holding a trencher, jesting merrily?
You put our page out. Go, you are allowed.
Die when you will, a smock shall be your shroud.   480
You leer upon me, do you? There's an eye
Wounds like a leaden sword.
BOYET.   Full merrily
Hath this brave manage, this career, been run.
BEROWNE. Lo, he is tilting straight. Peace! I have done.

461 *consent* agreement, conspiracy   463 *dash* heckle   464 *please-man* toady, yes man   464 *zany* stooge   465 *mumble-news* prattler, "big mouth"   465 *trencher-knight* parasite   465 *Dick* fellow (spoken contemptuously)   466 *in years* into wrinkles   470 *she* i.e., whom we intended to woo   473 *Much . . . 'tis* very much like this is the way it was   475 *my lady's . . . squier* by the square, by exact measurement, i.e., exactly how to appeal to her (spoken mockingly)   476 *upon the apple of her eye* very intimately with her   478 *trencher* plate   479 *out* i.e., of his part   479 *allowed* as a licensed or privileged fool   480 *smock* a woman's undergarment   482 *leaden* mock   483 *manage* horsemanship   483 *career* short gallop at full speed   484 *tilting straight* ready to attack with words immediately

Enter [Costard, the] Clown.

Welcome, pure wit! Thou part'st a fair fray.   485
COSTARD. O Lord, sir, they would know
   Whether the three Worthies shall come in or no.
BEROWNE. What, are there but three?
COSTARD.   No, sir; but it is vara fine,
   For every one pursents three.
BEROWNE.   And three times thrice is nine.
COSTARD. No so, sir, under correction, sir, I hope, it is
   not so.   490
   You cannot beg us, sir, I can assure you, sir; we know
   what we know:
   I hope, sir, three times thrice, sir—
BEROWNE.   Is not nine?
COSTARD. Under correction, sir, we know whereuntil it
   doth amount.
BEROWNE. By Jove, I always took three threes for nine.   495
COSTARD. O Lord, sir, it were pity you should get your
   living by reck'ning, sir.
BEROWNE. How much is it?
COSTARD. O Lord, sir, the parties themselves, the actors,
   sir, will show whereuntil it doth amount. For mine   500
   own part, I am, as they say, but to parfect one man
   in one poor man—Pompion the Great, sir.
BEROWNE. Art thou one of the Worthies?
COSTARD. It pleased them to think me worthy of Pompey
   the Great. For mine own part, I know not the degree   505
   of the Worthy, but I am to stand for him.
BEROWNE. Go, bid them prepare.
COSTARD. We will turn it finely off, sir; we will take some
   care.   *Exit.*
KING. Berowne, they will shame us. Let them not approach.

---

489 *pursents* i.e., represents   490, 493 *under correction* (disclaimer
to a superior for what is said)   491 *You cannot beg us* you cannot
make fools of us   501 *parfect* perform   502 *Pompion* Pompey;
pompion means "pumpkin"

BEROWNE. We are shame-proof, my lord; and 'tis some
      policy   51
   To have one show worse than the king's and his com-
      pany.

KING. I say they shall not come.

PRINCESS. Nay, my good lord, let me o'errule you now.
   That sport best pleases that doth least know how;
   Where zeal strives to content, and the contents   51
   Dies in the zeal of that which it presents.
   Their form confounded makes most form in mirth
   When great things laboring perish in their birth.

BEROWNE. A right description of our sport, my lord.

   - Enter [Armado, the] Braggart.

ARMADO. Anointed, I implore so much expense of thy   52
   royal sweet breath as will utter a brace of words.*
                  [*Converses with the King, and delivers
                              a paper to him.*]

PRINCESS. Doth this man serve God?

BEROWNE. Why ask you?

PRINCESS. 'A speaks not like a man of God his making.

ARMADO. That is all one, my fair, sweet, honey monarch;   52
   for, I protest, the schoolmaster is exceeding fantastical—too-too vain, too-too vain—but we will put it, as
   they say, to *fortuna de la guerra.* I wish you the peace
   of mind, most royal couplement!   *Exit.*

KING. Here is like to be a good presence of Worthies. He   53
   presents Hector of Troy; the swain, Pompey the Great;
   the parish curate, Alexander; Armado's page, Hercules; the pedant, Judas Maccabaeus:
   And if these four Worthies in their first show thrive,

514–16 *That sport . . . it presents* that entertainment is most pleasing which knows least how to entertain; in such entertainment zeal
strives to please, yet the performance perishes in its overzealousness
517–18 *Their form . . . their birth* "putting them out of form
mends the form of our mirth, when we see great things they aim'd
at come to nothing" (Capell)   519 *right* true   519 *our sport* i.e.,
disguise as Russians   528 *fortuna de la guerra* fortunes of war   529
couplement couple

These four will change habits and present the other
    five.   535
BEROWNE. There is five in the first show.
KING. You are deceivèd, 'tis not so.
BEROWNE. The pedant, the braggart, the hedge-priest,
    the fool, and the boy—
    Abate throw at novum, and the whole world again   540
    Cannot pick out five such, take each one in his vein.
KING. The ship is under sail, and here she comes amain.

    Enter [Costard armed, for] Pompey.

COSTARD. "I Pompey am—"
BEROWNE.   You lie, you are not he.
COSTARD. "I Pompey am—"
BOYET.   With libbard's head on knee.
BEROWNE. Well said, old mocker. I must needs be
    friends with thee.   545
COSTARD. "I Pompey am, Pompey surnamed the Big—"
DUMAINE. The "Great."
COSTARD. It is "Great," sir—"Pompey surnamed the
    Great;
    That oft in field, with targe and shield, did make my
      foe to sweat,
    And travelling along this coast, I here am come by
      chance,   550
    And lay my arms before the legs of this sweet lass of
      France."
    If your ladyship would say, "Thanks, Pompey," I had
      done.
PRINCESS. Great thanks, great Pompey.
COSTARD. 'Tis not so much worth; but I hope I was per-
    fect.
    I made a little fault in "Great."   555

538 *hedge-priest* (a contemptuous term for a mediocre priest who
preaches, as it were, under hedges along the road)   540 *Abate
throw at novum* except the throw at novum (a dicing game in
which the principal throws were nine and five)   544 *libbard's* leop-
ard's (line may allude to garments that bore insignia at elbows or
knees)   549 *targe* shield

BEROWNE. My hat to a halfpenny, Pompey proves the best Worthy.

Enter [Nathaniel, the] Curate for Alexander.

NATHANIEL. "When in the world I lived, I was the world's commander;
By east, west, north, and south, I spread my conquering might;
My scutcheon plain declares that I am Alisander—"   56(
(BOYET. Your nose says, no, you are not; for it stands too right.
BEROWNE. Your nose smells "no" in this, most tender-smelling knight.)

PRINCESS. The conqueror is dismayed. Proceed, good Alexander.

NATHANIEL. "When in the world I lived, I was the world's commander—"

BOYET. Most true, 'tis right: you were so, Alisander.   56ȝ

BEROWNE. Pompey the Great—

COSTARD. Your servant, and Costard.

BEROWNE. Take away the conqueror, take away Alisander.

COSTARD. [*to Nathaniel*] O, sir, you have overthrown Alisander the conqueror! You will be scraped out of   57(
the painted cloth for this. Your lion that holds his pollaxe sitting on a close-stool will be given to Ajax. He will be the ninth Worthy. A conqueror, and afeard to speak? Run away for shame, Alisander. [*Nathaniel retires.*] There, an 't shall please you, a foolish mild   575
man; an honest man, look you, and soon dashed. He is a marvellous good neighbor, faith, and a very good bowler; but for Alisander—alas, you see how 'tis—

---

561 *right* (it was well known that Alexander's head drooped towards his left side)   562 *Your nose . . . knight* (alludes to Alexander's reputation for a pleasant breath and odor)   571–72 *lion . . . close-stool* (Alexander traditionally bore insignia depicting a lion sitting in a chair, holding a battle-axe)   572 *close-stool* seat in a privy   572 *Ajax* the Greek hero; with pun on "a jakes," i.e., a privy

a little o'erparted. But there are Worthies a-coming
will speak their mind in some other sort.

PRINCESS. Stand aside, good Pompey.   580

    *Enter [Holofernes, the] Pedant for Judas, and
    [Moth,] the Boy for Hercules.*

HOLOFERNES. "Great Hercules is presented by this imp,
  Whose club killed Cerberus, that three-headed *canus*;
  And when he was a babe, a child, a shrimp,
  Thus did he strangle serpents in his *manus*.
  Quoniam he seemeth in minority,   585
  Ergo I come with this apology."
Keep some state in thy exit, and vanish.   *Exit Boy.*
"Judas I am—"
DUMAINE. A Judas!
HOLOFERNES. Not Iscariot, sir.   590
  "Judas I am, ycleped Maccabaeus."
DUMAINE. Judas Maccabaeus clipt is plain Judas.
BEROWNE. A kissing traitor. How, art thou proved Judas?
HOLOFERNES. "Judas I am—"
DUMAINE. The more shame for you, Judas.   595
HOLOFERNES. What mean you, sir?
BOYET. To make Judas hang himself.
HOLOFERNES. Begin, sir; you are my elder.
BEROWNE. Well followed: Judas was hanged on an elder.
HOLOFERNES. I will not be put out of countenance.   600
BEROWNE. Because thou hast no face.
HOLOFERNES. What is this?
BOYET. A cittern-head.

---

579 *o'erparted* given too demanding a role   582 *canus* dog   584
manus hands   585 *Quoniam* since   586 *Ergo* therefore   587 *state*
dignity   591 *ycleped* named   592 *Judas Maccabaeus* a Hebrew
warrier of the second century B.C.   592 *clipt* a triple quibble:
(1) on ycleped (2) on cutting down Judas Maccabaeus to "plain
Judas" (3) on the treacherous embrace of Jesus by Judas, hence a
"kissing traitor"   598–99 *you are . . . on an elder* (Holofernes'
mock deference is countered by reference to the tree, i.e., the elder,
upon which Judas was supposed to have hanged himself)   603
cittern-head the carved head on the neck of a cithern (form of
guitar)

DUMAINE. The head of a bodkin.

BEROWNE. A death's face in a ring.   605

LONGAVILLE. The face of an old Roman coin, scarce
seen.

BOYET. The pommel of Caesar's falchion.

DUMAINE. The carved-bone face on a flask.

BEROWNE. Saint George's half-cheek in a brooch.

DUMAINE. Ay, and in a brooch of lead.   610

BEROWNE. Ay, and worn in the cap of a toothdrawer.
And now forward, for we have put thee in countenance.

HOLOFERNES. You have put me out of countenance.

BEROWNE. False. We have given thee faces.

HOLOFERNES. But you have outfaced them all.   615

BEROWNE. An thou wert a lion, we would do so.

BOYET. Therefore as he is an ass, let him go.
And so adieu, sweet Jude. Nay, why dost thou stay?

DUMAINE. For the latter end of his name.

BEROWNE. For the ass to the Jude? Give it him, Jud-as,
away!   620

HOLOFERNES. This is not generous, not gentle, not
humble.

BOYET. A light for Monsieur Judas! It grows dark, he
may stumble.   [Holofernes retires.]

PRINCESS. Alas, poor Maccabaeus, how hath he been
baited!

Enter [Armado, the] Braggart [for Hector].

BEROWNE. Hide thy head, Achilles, here comes Hector
in arms.   625

DUMAINE. Though my mocks come home by me, I will
now be merry.

604 *bodkin* long pins with sculptured heads   605 *ring* i.e., one with
a death's-head   607 *falchion* sword   609 *half-cheek* profile   610
brooch of lead badge of trade   611 *worn in the cap of a toothdrawer* (badges were worn in hats to indicate trade, in this case, of
a toothdrawer, i.e., a primitive dentist)   626 *Though . . . by me*
(sense is obscure)

KING. Hector was but a Troyan in respect of this.
BOYET. But is this Hector?
KING. I think Hector was not so clean-timbered.   630
LONGAVILLE. His leg is too big for Hector's.
DUMAINE. More calf, certain.
BOYET. No; he is best indued in the small.
BEROWNE. This cannot be Hector.
DUMAINE. He's a god or a painter; for he makes faces.   635
ARMADO. "The armipotent Mars, of lances the almighty,
   Gave Hector a gift—"
DUMAINE. A gilt nutmeg.
BEROWNE. A lemon.
LONGAVILLE. Stuck with cloves.   640
DUMAINE. No, cloven.
ARMADO. Peace!
   "The armipotent Mars, of lances the almighty,
   Gave Hector a gift, the heir of Ilion;
   A man so breathed that certain he would fight, yea   645
   From morn till night, out of his pavilion."
   I am that flower—
DUMAINE.   That mint.
LONGAVILLE.   That columbine.
ARMADO. Sweet Lord Longaville, rein thy tongue.
LONGAVILLE. I must rather give it the rein, for it runs
   against Hector.   650
DUMAINE. Ay, and Hector's a greyhound.
ARMADO. The sweet war-man is dead and rotten. Sweet
   chucks, beat not the bones of the buried. When he
   breathed, he was a man. But I will forward with my

628 *Hector . . . of this* Hector was merely an ordinary fellow in
comparison to this, i.e., to Armado in his role of Hector   630
clean-timbered well-built   633 *small* the part of the leg below the
calf   636 *armipotent* mighty in arms   638–40 *gilt nutmeg . . .
cloves* (gilded nutmegs and oranges or lemons stuck with cloves
were valued as gifts and used in flavoring ale and wine)   645 *so
breathed* so full of breath, hence in good physical condition   646
pavilion ceremonial tent for a champion   651 *Hector's a greyhound* (Hector was a name often used for hounds)

device. Sweet royalty, bestow on me the sense of hear-   655
ing.   *Berowne steps forth.*

PRINCESS. Speak, brave Hector; we are much delighted.

ARMADO. I do adore thy sweet Grace's slipper.

BOYET. Loves her by the foot.

DUMAINE. He may not by the yard.   660

ARMADO. "This Hector far surmounted Hannibal.
        The party is gone."

COSTARD. Fellow Hector, she is gone.
        She is two months on her way.

ARMADO. What meanest thou?

COSTARD. Faith, unless you play the honest Troyan, the   665
        poor wench is cast away. She's quick; the child brags
        in her belly already: 'tis yours.

ARMADO. Dost thou infamonize me among potentates?
        Thou shalt die.

COSTARD. Then shall Hector be whipped for Jaquenetta   670
        that is quick by him, and hanged for Pompey that is
        dead by him.

DUMAINE. Most rare Pompey!

BOYET. Renowned Pompey!

BEROWNE. Greater than great. Great, great, great Pom-
        pey!   675
        Pompey the Huge!

DUMAINE. Hector trembles.

BEROWNE. Pompey is moved. More Ates, more Ates! Stir
        them on! stir them on!

DUMAINE. Hector will challenge him.   680

BEROWNE. Ay, if 'a have no more man's blood in his
        belly than will sup a flea.

ARMADO. By the north pole, I do challenge thee.

COSTARD. I will not fight with a pole, like a northern
        man. I'll slash; I'll do it by the sword. I bepray you,   685
        let me borrow my arms again.

656s.d. *Berowne steps forth* (evidently Berowne takes Costard aside
to prompt the report of Jaquenetta's supposed condition)   660
yard phallus (slang)   666 *quick* pregnant   666 *brags* by the enlargement of the belly   668 *infamonize* i.e., infamize, make me in-
famous   678 *Ates* spirits of discord   684 *pole* Costard's mistaking
of north pole(?) staff used by northern Englishmen(?)

DUMAINE. Room for the incensed Worthies!

COSTARD. I'll do it in my shirt.

DUMAINE. Most resolute Pompey!

MOTH. Master, let me take you a button-hole lower. Do   690
you not see, Pompey is uncasing for the combat?
What mean you? You will lose your reputation.

ARMADO. Gentlemen and soldiers, pardon me. I will not
combat in my shirt.

DUMAINE. You may not deny it. Pompey hath made the   695
challenge.

ARMADO. Sweet bloods, I both may and will.

BEROWNE. What reason have you for 't?

ARMADO. The naked truth of it is, I have no shirt. I go
woolward for penance.   700

BOYET. True, and it was enjoined him in Rome for want
of linen; since when, I'll be sworn he wore none but
a dishclout of Jaquenetta's, and that 'a wears next his
heart for a favor.

Enter a Messenger, Monsieur Marcade.

MARCADE. God save you, madam.   705

PRINCESS. Welcome, Marcade;
But that thou interrupt'st our merriment.

MARCADE. I am sorry, madam, for the news I bring
Is heavy in my tongue. The king your father—

PRINCESS. Dead, for my life!   710

MARCADE. Even so. My tale is told.

BEROWNE. Worthies, away! The scene begins to cloud.

ARMADO. For mine own part, I breathe free breath. I
have seen the day of wrong through the little hole of
discretion, and I will right myself like a soldier.   715
Exeunt Worthies.

---

690 *take . . . lower* (1) help you take off your doublet or jacket
(2) take you down a peg   691 *uncasing* undressing   700 *woolward*
for penance with woolen clothing against the skin to mortify the
flesh   713–15 *I have . . . discretion* I have realized my foolishness
through the understanding of others(?) I have realized that I have
been made a fool of, i.e., in accepting the story of Jaquenetta's
pregnancy(?)

KING. How fares your Majesty?

PRINCESS. Boyet, prepare. I will away to-night.

KING. Madam, not so. I do beseech you, stay.

PRINCESS. Prepare, I say. I thank you, gracious lords,
  For all your fair endeavors, and entreat,   720
  Out of a new-sad soul, that you vouchsafe
  In your rich wisdom to excuse or hide
  The liberal opposition of our spirits,
  If over-boldly we have borne ourselves
  In the converse of breath: your gentleness   725
  Was guilty of it. Farewell, worthy lord.
  A heavy heart bears not a humble tongue.
  Excuse me so, coming too short of thanks
  For my great suit so easily obtained.

KING. The extreme parts of time extremely forms   730
  All causes to the purpose of his speed,
  And often, at his very loose, decides
  That which long process could not arbitrate.
  And though the mourning brow of progeny
  Forbid the smiling courtesy of love   735
  The holy suit which fain it would convince,
  Yet, since love's argument was first on foot,
  Let not the cloud of sorrow justle it
  From what it purposed; since to wail friends lost
  Is not by much so wholesome-profitable   740
  As to rejoice at friends but newly found.

PRINCESS. I understand you not: my griefs are double.

BEROWNE. Honest plain words best pierce the ear of
    grief;

---

723 *liberal* excessively free   725 *converse of breath* conversation
725 *gentleness* courtesy   727 *humble* civil   729 *suit . . . obtained*
(refers to her father's claim, apparently satisfied by the King)
730–33 *The extreme . . . arbitrate* (the general sense is that the
pressure of time shapes matters to accord with the reasons for the
pressure and that often, at the critical moment, this pressure brings
about what a much longer time could not manage)   736 *which
fain it would convince* which gladly it, i.e., the smiling courtesy of
love, would prove   742 *double* one for father, one for departure
from King(?) (meaning is obscure)

And by these badges understand the king.
For your fair sakes have we neglected time,   745
Played foul play with our oaths. Your beauty, ladies,
Hath much deformed us, fashioning our humors
Even to the opposèd end of our intents;
And what in us hath seemed ridiculous—
As love is full of unbefitting strains,   750
All wanton as a child, skipping and vain,
Formed by the eye and therefore, like the eye,
Full of strange shapes, of habits and of forms,
Varying in subjects as the eye doth roll
To every varied object in his glance;   755
Which parti-coated presence of loose love
Put on by us, if, in your heavenly eyes,
Have misbecomed our oaths and gravities,
Those heavenly eyes that look into these faults
Suggested us to make. Therefore, ladies,   760
Our love being yours, the error that love makes
Is likewise yours. We to ourselves prove false,
By being once false for ever to be true
To those that make us both—fair ladies, you.
And even that falsehood, in itself a sin,   765
Thus purifies itself and turns to grace.
PRINCESS. We have received your letters, full of love;
Your favors, the ambassadors of love;
And in our maiden council rated them
At courtship, pleasant jest, and courtesy,   770
As bombast and as lining to the time.
But more devout than this in our respects
Have we not been, and therefore met your loves
In their own fashion, like a merriment.
DUMAINE. Our letters, madam, showed much more than
    jest.   775

---

744 *these badges* the tokens or "fairings" originally sent to the
ladies(?)   the recital of what follows(?)   748 *opposèd end* contrary aim   750 *strains* tendencies   756 *parti-coated* dressed in
motley, as a professional fool   760 *Suggested* tempted   769–70
rated them At estimated them to be merely   771 *bombast* pad-
ding   772 *devout* serious

LONGAVILLE. So did our looks.

ROSALINE.   We did not quote them so.

KING. Now, at the latest minute of the hour,
    Grant us your loves.

PRINCESS.   A time, methinks, too short
    To make a world-without-end bargain in.
    No, no, my lord, your Grace is perjured much,   780
    Full of dear guiltiness; and therefore this—
    If for my love (as there is no such cause)
    You will do aught, this shall you do for me:
    Your oath I will not trust, but go with speed
    To some forlorn and naked hermitage,   785
    Remote from all the pleasures of the world;
    There stay until the twelve celestial signs
    Have brought about the annual reckoning.
    If this austere insociable life
    Change not your offer made in heat of blood;   790
    If frosts and fasts, hard lodging and thin weeds,
    Nip not the gaudy blossoms of your love,
    But that it bear this trial, and last love;
    Then, at the expiration of the year,
    Come challenge me, challenge me by these deserts,   795
    And, by this virgin palm now kissing thine,
    I will be thine; and till that instant, shut
    My woeful self up in a mourning house,
    Raining the tears of lamentation
    For the remembrance of my father's death.   800
    If this thou do deny, let our hands part;
    Neither intitled in the other's heart.

KING. If this, or more than this, I would deny,
    To flatter up these powers of mine with rest,
    The sudden hand of death close up mine eye!   805
    Hence hermit then—my heart is in thy breast.

---

776 *quote* interpret   781 *dear* grievous   783 *aught* anything, i.e.,
I ask   787 *signs* i.e., of the zodiac   791 *weeds* garments   793 *last
love* continue as love   795 *these deserts* these deservings, i.e.,
worthy actions   802 *intitled* having a claim   804 *To flatter up . . .
rest* to coddle my natural energies with ease

BEROWNE. And what to me, my love? and what to me?

ROSALINE. You must be purgèd too; your sins are racked,
  You are attaint with faults and perjury;
  Therefore, if you my favor mean to get,   810
  A twelvemonth shall you spend, and never rest,
  But seek the weary beds of people sick.

DUMAINE. But what to me, my love? but what to me?
  A wife?

KATHARINE.   A beard, fair health, and honesty;
  With three-fold love I wish you all these three.   815

DUMAINE. O, shall I say "I thank you, gentle wife"?

KATHARINE. Not so, my lord. A twelvemonth and a
  day
  I'll mark no words that smooth-faced wooers say.
  Come when the king doth to my lady come;
  Then, if I have much love, I'll give you some.   820

DUMAINE. I'll serve thee true and faithfully till then.

KATHARINE. Yet swear not, lest ye be forsworn again.

LONGAVILLE. What says Maria?

MARIA.   At the twelvemonth's end
  I'll change my black gown for a faithful friend.

LONGAVILLE. I'll stay with patience, but the time is long. 825

MARIA. The liker you—few taller are so young.

BEROWNE. Studies my lady? Mistress, look on me.
  Behold the window of my heart, mine eye,
  What humble suit attends thy answer there.
  Impose some service on me for thy love.   830

ROSALINE. Oft have I heard of you, my Lord Berowne,
  Before I saw you; and the world's large tongue
  Proclaims you for a man replete with mocks,
  Full of comparisons and wounding flouts,
  Which you on all estates will execute   835

807–12 *And what . . . sick* (most editors bracket lines 807–812;
these verses appear to be part of a first draft which failed to be
removed, for Berowne makes another request of Rosaline at line
829)   808 *racked* put on the rack, i.e., tortured and made to con-
fess(?)   826 *liker* more like   834 *comparisons* sarcastic similes
834 *flouts* gibes, "digs"   835 *estates* classes of people

That lie within the mercy of your wit.
To weed this wormwood from your fruitful brain,
And therewithal to win me, if you please—
Without the which I am not to be won—
You shall this twelvemonth term from day to day   840
Visit the speechless sick, and still converse
With groaning wretches; and your task shall be
With all the fierce endeavor of your wit
To enforce the painèd impotent to smile.

BEROWNE. To move wild laughter in the throat of death?   845
It cannot be; it is impossible:
Mirth cannot move a soul in agony.

ROSALINE. Why, that's the way to choke a gibing spirit,
Whose influence is begot of that loose grace
Which shallow laughing hearers give to fools.   850
A jest's prosperity lies in the ear
Of him that hears it, never in the tongue
Of him that makes it. Then, if sickly ears,
Deafed with the clamors of their own dear groans,
Will hear your idle scorns, continue then,   855
And I will have you and that fault withal;
But if they will not, throw away that spirit,
And I shall find you empty of that fault,
Right joyful of your reformation.

BEROWNE. A twelvemonth? Well, befall what will befall,   860
I'll jest a twelvemonth in an hospital.

PRINCESS. [to the King] Ay, sweet my lord; and so I take
my leave.

KING. No, madam; we will bring you on your way.

BEROWNE. Our wooing doth not end like an old play;
Jack hath not Jill. These ladies' courtesy   865
Might well have made our sport a comedy.

KING. Come, sir, it wants a twelvemonth and a day,
And then 'twill end.

BEROWNE.   That's too long for a play.

    Enter [Armado, the] Braggart.

844 *painèd impotent* suffering helpless ones

ARMADO. Sweet majesty, vouchsafe me—
PRINCESS. Was not that Hector?   870
DUMAINE. The worthy knight of Troy.
ARMADO. I will kiss thy royal finger, and take leave. I am
   a votary; I have vowed to Jaquenetta to hold the
   plough for her sweet love three year. But, most esteemed greatness will you hear the dialogue that the   875
   two learned men have compiled in praise of the owl
   and the cuckoo? It should have followed in the end
   of our show.
KING. Call them forth quickly; we will do so.
ARMADO. Holla! approach.

   Enter all.

   This side is *Hiems*, Winter; this *Ver*, the Spring; the   880
   one maintained by the owl, th' other by the cuckoo.
   Ver, begin.

                     The Song.*

[*Spring.*]   When daisies pied and violets blue
                   And lady-smocks all silver-white
               And cuckoo-buds of yellow hue   885
                   Do paint the meadows with delight,
               The cuckoo then, on every tree,
               Mocks married men; for thus sings he,
                                        Cuckoo;
               Cuckoo, cuckoo: O, word of fear,   890
               Unpleasing to a married ear!

               When shepherds pipe on oaten straws,
                   And merry larks are ploughmen's clocks,
               When turtles tread, and rooks, and daws,
                   And maidens bleach their summer smocks,   895

---

875 *dialogue* debate   880–81 *the one . . . the cuckoo* the one side
of the debate taken by the owl, the other side by the cuckoo
884–85 *lady-smocks . . . cockoo-buds* varieties of watercresses or
cuckoo flowers   894 *turtles tread* turtledoves mate

The cuckoo then, on every tree,
Mocks married men; for thus sings he,
                                        Cuckoo;
Cuckoo, cuckoo: O, word of fear,
Unpleasing to a married ear!   900

Winter.   When icicles hang by the wall,
                  And Dick the shepherd blows his nail,
              And Tom bears logs into the hall,
                  And milk comes frozen home in pail,
              When blood is nipped, and ways be foul,   905
              Then nightly sings the staring owl,
                                        Tu-who;
              Tu-whit, tu-who: a merry note,
              While greasy Joan doth keel the pot.

              When all aloud the wind doth blow,   910
                  And coughing drowns the parson's saw,
              And birds sit brooding in the snow,
                  And Marian's nose looks red and raw,
              When roasted crabs hiss in the bowl,
              Then nightly sings the staring owl,   915
                                        Tu-who;
              Tu-whit, tu-who: a merry note,
              While greasy Joan doth keel the pot.

ARMADO. The words of Mercury are harsh after the songs
of Apollo. You, that way: we, this way.   920
                                    *Exeunt omnes.**

---

902 *blows his nail* stands about idly   909 *keel* cool by stirring,
skimming, or pouring on something cold   911 *saw* saying   914
crabs crab apples

Director's Preparation
and Production Notes

Director's Preparation
and Production Notes

I. i. 32 The King turned to his third companion, calling, "Berowne!"

36–37 As Berowne said, "But there are other strict observances:/ As not to see a woman in that term," I had the female statue removed and the telescope replace it as the central decorative item on the stage.

49 As the servants took away the badminton rackets and creature comforts, they substituted huge piles of books, ostensibly for study.

177 s.d. *Enter [Dull]*. His few scenes, coupled together, seem to indicate a man who is not all there—literally. He is often in scenes without "being" there, without having a line. One tries to find a characterization that will encompass some reason to make him stay on the scene without saying a word. The actor and I together developed a character who was rather slow-witted and had a very short span of attention.

177 s.d. *Enter [Dull]* . . . Costard evaded Dull by very neatly slipping out of his jerkin, and immediately one got the impression of him as a sly, quicksilver type of character. As he did this, however, he ran into Berowne and was caught again. Costard was thus seen at once as someone who is always trying to weasel out of situations that he gets into, but who always gets caught.

297 s.d. *Exeunt.* Just to add a final fillip to the

scene and to their relationship, I had Costard try to escape from Berowne. He was given a huge pile of books to carry out for Berowne; he managed to dump the books back into Berowne's lap and scamper off, only to run into Dull, the Constable, who had been "dully" waiting outside for him; and as he turned to escape from the Constable, he walked smack into Berowne, who dumped the books back into his arms, and the three of them went off together.

I. ii. As often happens in *Love's Labor's Lost*, the comic theme in this scene, relating to love, directly parallels the main plot. Don Armado falls hopelessly in love with Jaquenetta, just as Berowne does with Rosaline. How interesting that we see Armado's comic, distorted, and farcical exploration of the love theme before we see the lyric exploration of Berowne. It is almost as if by seeing the comic inversion first, we are asked to take the other less seriously.

1 As an element of character, the actor playing Don Armado came to use a lisp, not because we were looking for ways to make Don Armado funny, or because we were worried about getting laughs for the character, but because a Castilian lisp fitted in with Armado's pretensions to grandeur. It was also a popular language joke on the Elizabethan stage. In our production, the gentle Castilian lisp had both charm and humor.

3 In the character of Moth, the brightness and quickness of mind are so important that I cast not a boy, but a slightly older actor, a young man who looked as though he might be thirteen or fourteen, in order not to lose the verbal nature and precision of the comedy. Although I have seen Moth played with great charm by a young child, the scene never achieves the quickness and sharpness of intellect and wit that it de-

mands without a talented actor, in which case
the character of Armado suffers, as well as the
scene.

122 Moth substituted himself for Jaquenetta without
Dull's realizing this. On "Fare you well," Dull
dragged Moth offstage. At line 134, Dull realized
his mistake, howled a cry of recognition offstage,
and re-entered for Jaquenetta.

II. i.   I wanted to see the Princess and her retinue
arrive in a boat. In an outdoor theater like the
Delacorte, I always feel elements of spectacle
are desirable when the play allows for it. There
is a lake directly behind the stage area, and I
conceived of a huge sail and mast gliding into
view and the ladies disembarking from their
vessel, accompanied by a flurry of activity—
servants coming down to welcome them and
take their trunks. However, we had budget trou-
bles at the time, and so my dream boat became
an offstage coach announced by a post horn.

1   Boyet might be thought of as a version of Don
Armado—someone with true intellect, education, and real birthright, but a figure of fun because he takes himself too seriously. Throughout
the play I see various characters fragmented and
splintered, as if there were a mirror called *Love's
Labor's Lost* which fell to the ground and shat-
tered. In the slivers I see different aspects of the
characters reflected. In some ways Costard is a
reflection of Berowne, and even Don Armado is
a reflection of Berowne; and here I see Boyet
as a reflection of Don Armado.

130 Navarre was portrayed as a nearsighted man, but
again this was not used as a gag or in a farcical
way. The occasional use of his glasses gave him
a slightly professorial attitude, which was in
keeping with his scholarly leanings and resolu-
tions about establishing an "academe" and his

ideas about the life to be led there. At this point,
it seemed quite natural for the King to put on
his glasses in order to study the document a little
more closely. As he did so, he suddenly saw the
Princess clearly for the first time and indicated
that he was keenly affected by her charms. Then,
as he looked back at the document, he suddenly
became aware that he was wearing glasses, which
he thought made him less attractive. As he
whipped off the glasses, one understood how
love is a trigger to vanity.

188   When Rosaline said, "No point, with my knife,"
she used her fan or her finger to make a sharp
jabbing thrust at Berowne, as if to say "keep
your distance" and thoroughly discourage him,
knowing at the same time, of course, that the
spirit of the gesture would attract and encourage
him. He turned with great self-confidence to
leave, but as he did so, he tripped, which delighted Rosaline and cued her line, "And yours
from long living" (190). His response, "I cannot
stay thanksgiving" (191), although meant ironi-
cally, referred to the departure of the others—
Dumaine, Longaville, and the King—conveying
Berowne's fear that his delay would be noticed
if it were extended. He ran off.

249 ff.   Their departure took the form of a "game"
exit, like hide-and-go-seek, a game of "who is
'it'?" or tag. And so, whirling and twirling, as if
they were out for fun and the fun would continue offstage and throughout the day, they left
the stage.

III. i. 3   Moth crowed the word "Concolinel" several
times.

6   How interesting that Shakespeare again parallels
the moral breakdown of the four suitors with
Armado here in this scene. (I now realize how
accurate it is to characterize Armado as a thing

of shreds and patches. Armado is an absolute shambles of a character.) He poses as a great moralist and someone of tremendous integrity, but he is the one who first breaks the code. In spite of his pretense, how susceptible he is to his passions of the flesh! He is still a character of gentle humor as opposed to Costard's lustier approach to humor, but they are essentially in the same mold.

9 Here is another instance where I considered a cut, because Moth's speech seemed long and difficult to understand. But in dealing with this section on the stage, the speech turned out to be a little aria, as it were, a little *tour de force* for the character of Moth. The actor was able to clarify the rather difficult words with mimicry and mime so that the speech turned out to be a very delightful moment, instead of awkward or obscure.

25–29 The majority of the audience probably did not understand the bawdy references, even though the actors did some illustration of the points. More important, however, the actors themselves had a clear idea of the interchange and were able to communicate the general fun of it. This sustained the audience until the section that it could more readily understand, beginning with, "A man, if I live; and this, by, in, and without, upon the instant" (35–36).

63 On "Here's a costard," Costard struck his own shin onstage. At line 65, he rubbed his shin.

95 As he said, "cunning as fast and loose," Costard made a break for it, only to be stopped by Armado. Once again, he confused Armado with double-talk, and before you knew it, he was out again: "I, Costard, running out, that was safely within,/ Fell over the threshold and broke my shin" (108–109).

128 "Now will I look to his remuneration. Remuner-

ation? O that's the Latin word for three farthings." I had Costard adopt an attitude of
cynicism about the low value of the tip. In trying to find a contemporary image that would
make the character of Costard vivid to the actor,
I suggested that he was like a New York cab
driver. For example, it doesn't matter what you
give a cab driver, it's always too little—and
he'll thank you for nothing. This spirit pervaded
Costard's speech and was delivered in like
manner.

159 Costard responds with appreciation and delight
to Berowne's sizable tip.

IV. i. 70 Since Armado's writing form had been ex-
ploited earlier by the Duke (I. i. 213 ff.), and
this letter seemed to have less fun in it than the
first one, I cut the lines, "He came, one; saw,
two; overcame, three. Who came? The king . . . ,"
etc., through line 78 ("thou the beggar, for so
witnesseth thy lowliness."). The point of the
letter seemed to have been made by line 69 and
was being overmade in the following section.
Perhaps, through no fault of the actors' lively
invention, we never found the correct action for
this letter.

82–86 The lines from, "Thus, expecting thy reply,"
through "Don Adriano de Armado" were given
to Rosaline. The decision to alternate the lines
of the letter and the subsequent little poem between Boyet and Rosaline came out of the actors' invention in keeping alive their relationship.
The impulse of the actress playing Rosaline,
when she was being kidded, was to snatch the
letter from Boyet's hands to make him stop
reading it and to mitigate her embarrassment
by taking part in the joke, by reading the letter
herself. Without doing violation to the text, it
seemed to keep the spirit of "games" alive.

89–92 Despite having worked with these lines for a long time during the rehearsal period, we could find no way to keep them alive and fresh, and therefore we cut them. Boyet's point was made when he used the first two lines to joke with Rosaline.

95–96 The cut connected the Princess' questions, "What vane? What weathercock?" directly to Boyet's line, "This Armado is a Spaniard that keeps here in court," thus clarifying the sequence for the audience.

124–127 These verses were sung as if they belonged to a familiar ditty.

127 Katharine and Rosaline departed together, leaving Maria to cope with Boyet.

IV. ii. 11 I think it is virtually impossible to communicate the play on the word "credo" to a modern audience. What the actors do have to work with are the relationships between Holofernes, Nathaniel, and Dull. Dull's belligerence, Holofernes' pedantry and superiority, and Nathaniel's sycophantic attitude of protection and snobbery can be projected, and it is on this level —of character—that the material works.

23 Although most people grasp the sense of Nathaniel's speech, beginning "Sir, he hath never fed of the dainties that are bred in a book," this understanding is not essential to the fun. The fun is in Nathaniel's patronizing attitude toward Dull.

34 The humor in Dull's riddle ("What was a month old at Cain's birth that's not five weeks old as yet?") and all of the following riddles and jokes about the moon and Dictynna may have made more sense in Elizabethan times, but again, the attitudes of the characters—their confusion, their pomposity, their verbosity—all suffice to clarify these moments for a present-day audience.

52 One of the funniest moments occurred when Holofernes invited himself to extemporize on the death of the deer. The humor came out of the actor's delivery of the words, the vowel sounds that were strung together, and the ridiculousness of the poem.

70–77 These lines contain many lewd references. We discovered that Holofernes, in addition to being a pompous and arrogant pedant, was also a lecher. How fitting, how marvelous, to put the appetites of a *bon vivant* into the robes of a pedant.

82 Seeing the lecherous intent of Holofernes, Costard took an apple that he was chewing and shoved it in the schoolmaster's mouth at the end of the line, ". . . he that is likest to a hogshead." Holofernes, being the butt of this joke, removed the apple and belittled Costard with a contemptuous epithet on his size and intellect.

86–140 In rehearsal, this section seemed obscure at first but soon found its own natural life. Basically, Holofernes is trying to seduce Jaquenetta, Nathaniel is trying to impress Holofernes, and Costard is looking to make a buck without losing Jaquenetta. The action was as follows: As Nathaniel perused the letter, Holofernes took the opportunity to draw Jaquenetta aside under the guise of educating her or making small talk, while Nathaniel was reading, and Dull and Costard were trying to see the contents of the letter. Holofernes used his fake Latin and phony references to impress and entice Jaquenetta aside. As he recited the little Latin quote (89), he tapped it out on Jaquenetta's ample bosom as if he were reading it off a copy book. He became more and more familiar, in a madcap way, all but plunging down her low neckline. He remained carried away by the euphoria induced

by Jaquenetta's physical presence until Nathaniel, who had finally finished the letter, saw what
was going on and, with a clearing of the throat,
called Holofernes back to decorum. In an attempt to recover his dignity, Holofernes said,
"Under pardon, sir, what are the contents?
or, rather, as Horace says in his—" (95–97).
Unfortunately, Holofernes had no idea what
Horace said at *any* time so he covered the embarrassing moment by snatching the letter from
Nathaniel. Then, after quickly perusing it in an
offhand, authoritative way, he bade Nathaniel
read it aloud. Nathaniel took advantage of the
moment to impress Holofernes with a small performance. He read it with loving care and great
expression. Costard, who attempted to be interested for a while, began to nod out of boredom.
Dull had long since fallen asleep. While Nathaniel's attention was wholly on the performance of the letter, Holofernes used the relative
privacy of the moment to stroll with Jaquenetta
upstage. As they came to the area of the
fountain, the actor took advantage of the telescope prop and began to show Jaquenetta the
wonders of the instrument, using it to get his
arms around her, much as lovers do today on top
of the Empire State Building. Being a man given
to excesses, Holofernes went to the other end of
the telescope to get a better look at Jaquenetta's
heavenly beauties. Nathaniel suddenly became
aware that nobody was listening to him, and
broke off his reading, catching Holofernes in
the act. Holofernes immediately covered up his
antics by pompously and rather aggressively
carrying on as if he had been listening all the
time and implying that the fault, whatever it
was, was Nathaniel's. This is typical of Holofernes' behavior and may be summed up as,

"When in the wrong, attack." Holofernes continually attacks everyone and everything in sight, insulting them and putting them down and bashing out at their inadequacies.

157   Nathaniel and Holofernes started off and, as an afterthought, invited Dull to join them. He had been fast asleep during the last part of the scene. There may be another solution to what Dull is doing during the last half of the scene, but I do not know what it is, since he is silent for so long.

IV. iii. 1 s.d.   We did not follow the stage direction. Berowne did not have "a paper in his hand."

30–33   These lines were cut from the King's poem— an arbitrary cut dictated by the length of the poem.

48–49   ". . . the corner-cap of society,/ The shape of love's Tyburn" was cut. It was an obscure reference that confused the image. "Thou mak'st the triumviry, . . . that hangs up simplicity," kept the meter, and is the sense of the line.

62–66   These lines of Longaville's poem were cut because of length. The audience did not appreciate the inside, stylistic jokes of the poems themselves, jokes of construction and prosody. The fun came from certain more obvious delineations of the poems, such as the shallowness that we brought out in the King's poem. The pedantic and unoriginal metrics and slavish rhyming of Longaville's poem were emphasized in the actor's reading of it.

285   The important thing in this long, long discourse of Berowne is to keep it alive, and not assume that it is just one set speech. Here again, because it is so long and seems redundant, the tendency is to do some cutting. Much of it is not necessary, literally, but it is rich in its variety, beautifully constructed, and very amusing. The boys

want to be convinced that what they are doing is right. They want some moral justification for breaking their oaths, and Berowne has the problem of convincing them (286–327). He is thinking on his feet—he actually does not know what he is going to say—but they are listening expectantly, although they give him some resistance to sharpen and test his arguments. The speech has a quasi-legal form: a presentation of ideas, a recapitulation and extension of them, and then a summing up (345–349). Rather than being redundant, it is a form that reinforces the humor.

327 Line 327 is like an introduction, and the song proper begins on line 329 ("A lover's eyes will gaze an eagle blind"). I used music to underscore this rhapsody, only to intensify what it already is—a love song. I had all four of the men lean on each other. They feel, they experience, they dream, they fantasize collectively. They soothe and heal the rupture of oaths and friendship. They are surrendering to their natural passions with this shared "song."

350 "Then fools you were these women to forswear," is an abrupt change and the beginning of the climax to Berowne's argument. In a kind of coda, he summons them with a call to arms. On line 361 the King says, ". . . soldiers, to the field!" Berowne says, "Advance your standards. . . ." And they are a united army serving a common general, Love. Their progress can be followed thus: first, there was the presentation and winning of the argument; then the rhapsodizing on the theme; and finally, there was the call to arms that led to a plan of action—all quite silly and sophomoric, but also charming and delightful.

372–375 Note that he says, "We will with some strange pastime solace them,/ Such as the shortness of the time can shape;/ For revels, dances, masks, and merry hours/ Forerun fair Love. . . ." These were the clues I used to shape the entertainment in the second act of our production, which starts with the stage direction, "Enter Blackamoors with music" (V. ii. 157).

381 In every way I tried to reinforce the mock battle plan. They posed as soldiers; they assumed patriotic attitudes; at the end, they marched off in military fashion to a mock march played on harpsichord and drum.

V. i. 15 s.d.   The stage direction, "Draw out his table-book," led us to use the table-book as a prop for Nathaniel throughout the play. From time to time, he would write down the very stupid and malaprop sentences of Holofernes as if they were imperishable maxims to be recorded.

27 Holofernes rapped Nathaniel on the knuckles after "Priscian a little scratched," as he would a schoolboy.

31–32 Armado says, "Chirrah!" Holofernes says, confidentially to Nathaniel, "*Quare* 'chirrah,' not 'sirrah'?" as if to say, "You see what airs Armado affects?" Following our previous decision to have Armado affect a Castilian accent, "ch" was pronounced "thirrah," so Holofernes' criticism, "Quare 'thirrah,' not 'sirrah'?" made sense. It seems likely to me that this was Shakespeare's original intention, although there may be a reason for the "ch" that we never discovered.

49 In Holofernes' "*Quis, quis,* thou consonant," "thou consonant" was directed at Moth in an insulting and pejorative tone. Moth, unruffled, converted the insult to a quip.

64–68 There was some editing of Costard's speech in order to move the scene along. The lines,

"Hold, there is the very remuneration I had of thy master" and "O, an the heavens were so pleased that thou wert but my bastard, what a joyful father wouldest thou make me!" were cut. The lines are amusing, however, and might work in another production.

85 ff. Armado's long speech was amusing, because while Armado put on airs, Holofernes and Nathaniel mocked him behind his back with critical looks and comments.

131 Armado delivered his line, "Shall I tell you a thing?" with great suspense and enthusiasm, as if there were a very special pronouncement to follow. His next line, "We will have, if this fadge not, an antic," was such an anticlimax that it produced a laugh.

135 During the whole scene, Dull had fallen asleep, as usual, and it was only when Holofernes called to him that he woke up and danced off with the others.

V. ii. 3 Notice that the Princess only mentions the diamonds she received from the king. Rosaline asks, "Madam, came nothing else along with that?" (5), and as the Princess says, "Nothing but this?" and then confesses to a poem, I presumed they were playing a game, and that Rosaline was teasing the Princess.

9 After the Princess said, "That he was fain to seal on Cupid's name," I had Rosaline snatch the poem from her hand and start to read it. The Princess tried to retrieve the poem and chased Rosaline around the stage. The other girls kept the Princess from Rosaline, so that the chase became a game of keep-away.

10–14 "That was the way to make his godhead wax," is a sexual reference, and Rosaline's line, " 'a killed your sister" referred to the Princess but was directed at Katharine. In the line, "He made her melancholy, sad, and heavy," "heavy" was taken to mean pregnant.

42　In looking for some way to make this amusing to a modern audience, I interpreted the letter *B* to mean the profile of a pregnant woman, the top of the *B* representing the breast and the bottom of the *B*, the full belly. Katharine illustrated this with good humor, without any attempt to be lewd or bawdy.

44　"My red dominical" led me to think that perhaps Katharine was a redhead. In our production, to help distinguish one girl from another, Maria was a blonde, Katharine was red-haired, Rosaline was black-haired (see line 41) and the Princess was brown-haired. The Princess is referred to in the text as fair but I interpreted this in terms of grace and deportment rather than coloring.

44-46　". . . my golden letter./ O, that your face were not so full of O's!/ A pox of that jest, and I beshrew all shrows!" was cut; it seemed to suggest the exchange between Katharine and Rosaline was continuing from the previous argument (20–28).

54　The shape of each paper was different. The Princess' poem was written on quite a large sheet that had been folded into a very small triangle; Katharine's message looked like a round fan made up of flower petals; Maria's poem was upon a long scroll, which she unrolled when she said the line, "This letter is too long by half a mile."

70-72　"Folly, in wisdom hatched," and the next lines through the end of 72, were cut to make the first statement clearer.

77-78　These lines were given to Katharine.

127　We used full face masks on center sticks so that the ladies could hide their faces completely from

the men and still reveal them to the audience so
that it might see their reactions.

157 s.d. *Enter Blackamoors.* A problem arose in
trying to give a Russian flavor to the music and
yet keep within the Elizabethan tonal range. The
composer used a balalaika, mandolin, oboe, flute,
harpsichord, and percussion.

180 A Russian accent was used by Berowne and then
taken up by the other men. It seemed a natural
follow-through of the disguises.

194 Confused, the king answered, "Da!", then turned
to his companions for help.

212 Rosaline says, "Play, music then." The music
started. They all raised a foot as if to dance, but
Rosaline interrupted: "Not yet—no dance!",
and the music stopped, leaving the men with
their feet suspended in air. A few lines later, I
had the music start again, and it continued
softly under the scene. The rest of the scene was
staged as a kind of dance, with couples moving
in formal patterns. (See "Directing *Love's
Labor's Lost*, V. ii.)

251 The purpose of this little scene was to make
Longaville appear clumsy. Our key was taken
from the line, ". . . it may prove an ox." The
remainder of the conversation was cut; we found
no way of coping with it.

280–282 I cut these lines simply to move the scene
in a more direct manner. We went straight from
Katharine's line, "Lord Longaville said I came
o'er his heart; . . ." (279), to Rosaline's rejoinder
on line 283, "But will you hear? The king is my
love sworn."

328–330 These lines were also cut to help the flow
of the scene.

338–339 Berowne's "See where it comes! Behavior,
what wert thou,/ Till this madman showed thee?
and what art thou now?" would seem to express
Shakespeare's idea of how Boyet should re-enter;

Boyet should no doubt overplay it, to set up what is to come. In our production, therefore, Boyet added extra flourishes to his gestures and grandiloquence to his tone.

521 As the entertainment began, footmen brought in many candelabra to hang on the set in order to give the scene a festive feeling.

883 I divided up the song to give it interest and to keep it amongst principal characters, *i.e.*, Holofernes, Moth, Jaquenetta, Costard. And as the song progressed from Winter to Spring, the melody went from a major to a minor key, and the accompaniment became more and more emotional and wistful.

920 Armado also spoke the stage direction at the end—"Exeunt omnes."

Notes on Costumes, Sets, and Music

Notes on Costumes, Sets, and Music

COSTUMES

There is something very decorative about this play. It exudes stylishness and artifice in language and structure—I suppose because at first reading it seems to be about nothing really but the game of love, and it is played in an attractive setting by the most attractive, yet somewhat foolish and lovable, young people. I thought the clothes must be particularly beautiful to look at as well as functional. The dazzle of the clothes echoes the surface dazzle of the play. It seemed a necessity and not just a luxury.

I chose to set the decor of the play in the late Elizabethan period. It was not necessary that the clothes be historically accurate, but in terms of a general silhouette and series of details, they had to readily suggest Shakespeare's own period, as I feel the play is uniquely of his time. The Court of Navarre is redolent of nothing so much as an English country house, which is peopled on its fringes by a Costard, Jaquenetta, Dull, Nathaniel, and Holofernes, of whom there are no greater English prototypes.

I wanted the characters to appear at first rather stiff and formal and gradually break down and come apart to reveal more of the human being. Their dress served as a kind of armor, shielding the vulnerable person beneath. The colors went from more somber shades to lighter shades as the play progressed. The men first appeared in deep rose and royal purple, blue, and dusty green, and stiff doublets and ruffs. On first meeting the ladies, this sober image was augmented by wearing large, cumbersome hats. In this way, the costumes reflected the formality of both the language and the structure in the opening scenes of the play, in which the rhymed couplets and strongly metered verse suggest a certain stiffness.

Gradually, the artifice of language found in the beginning becomes less formal and more personal. The ascetic task to which the young men are dedicating themselves is subverted by romance, and it has the effect of relaxing and easing their minds and bodies to make way for the pursuit of passion and pleasure. As the men's passion grew, they began to remove various articles of clothing, which served to soften the outline of their persons. First the hats went, and then off came the doublets, and by Act IV, scene iii, they appeared very Byronic in full sleeves, open-throated shirts and knee breeches, looking much more like young boys than men.

The ladies, although essentially Elizabethan in silhouette, were softened in color and detail, and a subtle monochromatic pairing with their male partner made the couples' identification a little clearer from the start. They were also required to be as feminine and seductive as possible, but seductive by being all covered up. The modesty of costume not only suggested hidden delights, but also conformed to the more formal feeling of the beginning.

There was a complete change of costume in our second act, and there would have been more had the budget allowed. The clothes were softer and more relaxed in silhouette and detail. Materials ranged from the stiff brocades of the first act to soft satins and chiffon. High necks and stiff collars gave way to V-necks for the men and decolletage for the women. The instinct of the sexes to entice, flatter, and enhance was being expressed in every detail. Both men and ladies were dressed in very light, pastel colors that were obviously impractical and luxurious. This was also intended to offset and highlight the element of seriousness at the end of the play. I have discussed the effect of this last scene previously (see Introduction to "Directing *Love's Labor's Lost*") and it truly is key to all decisions. The very high fashion and superficiality of the clothes become shabby when compared to the deeply human and essential values that emerge at the end. The contrast must be made apparent.

The Russian disguises were based on Elizabethan drawings of Muscovite ambassadors. They needed no exaggeration in detail, as they were enormously theatrical and contrasted strongly to the English Elizabethan apparel.

SETS

In creating a set I ask myself first, what are the physical requirements of the play? These are usually dictated by the most demanding scene in terms of physical action or the intricacies of simultaneous scenes. I can usually select this scene after a few readings of the play, viewing the play through my imaginative resources. It soon became clear that Act IV, scene iii, made the most demands on the setting. I needed four areas, which might conceivably hide one character from the other and yet reveal them all to the audience at the same time. This seemed to dictate an "above" area with stairs leading to it.

All the references in the play are about a park and open fields, since the King is expressly forbidden by his edict to let ladies enter his castle. But this outdoor area seemed to call for a manicured setting in order to encompass the formal meeting of the King and Princess and the entertainment of the last scene. This in turn began to suggest a center fountain which, although outdoors, would still be decorative and suggest formality, and serve as a useful sitting place to create the needed levels for the staging. The fountain also served to edge the actors downstage toward the audience, and it created a realistic obstacle to force movement logically into a circular pattern which I felt would be appropriate for the material. The movement became more decorative than direct, and more graceful than literal.

The set as finally designed served the most demanding scene, IV. iii., admirably. Berowne came in center stage; he heard the King offstage begin to read, and quickly hid behind the stairs. Later, to get a better vantage point, he crept up the stairs into the cupola above. The King first hid behind the fountain in the center as Longaville entered and then stole behind the stairs. When Dumaine came in, Longaville hid on the fore-steps, in front of the stage.

Although I once considered a checkerboard floor to reinforce the "games" atmosphere of the play and, at another time, two balanced pavilions, which would be self-contained establishments to house the warring sexes, I discarded these ideas, as they only represented a part of Shakespeare's theme.

The nature of the specific details evolved from a discussion of period decor, and the designer's choice and imagination. Once having decided on Elizabethan as the period, the choices were obviously limited. The first problem was to create a sense of lightness and effervescence that would be suitable to the play and also contain recognizable elements of the Tudor period. I suggested that the designer take the ornate and decorative interior of a Tudor palace and remove the walls, as it were, leaving the carved tracery. Another demand on the designer was the creation of a symmetrical form to complement the balanced elements of the play's structure.

MUSIC

The music for *Love's Labor's Lost* had to blend with the other production elements. So it in turn had to be delicate and effervescent, warm and comic, and also suggest the Elizabethan period. The instrumentation was limited to the sounds contained in Elizabethan instruments, such as strings and woodwinds. The strongest "color" element was the use of a harpsichord. The most difficult problem was composing a vigorous and lusty Russian dance that still kept within this texture. The addition of the unique balalaika sound did much to solve this problem.

Basically, the music was used for segues between scenes. An overture helped set the tone for the beginning of the production, and the closing song reinforced the sweet and poignant mood at the end of the play. On only two occasions was music used as a lyric underpinning for a soliloquy, and in both cases I felt that Shakespeare had in effect created a song and I wished to strengthen that impression. The first was Boyet's speech in Act II, scene i (234–247), and the second, Berowne's rhapsody in Act IV, scene iii (329–349).

Reference List

Reference List

RECENT EDITIONS OF *Love's Labor's Lost*

A New Variorum Edition, ed. Horace H. Furness. Philadel-
phia: J. B. Lippincott Co., 1904. Paperback reprint. New
York: Dover, 1964.

The Arden Edition, ed. H. C. Hart. London: Methuen and
Co., Ltd., 1906. Revised edition, ed. Richard David (1951).

The New Cambridge Edition, ed. A. Quiller-Couch and J. D.
Wilson. Cambridge, England: Cambridge University Press,
1923. Revised edition, ed. J. D. Wilson (1962).

The Yale Shakespeare Edition, ed. W. L. Cross and C. F.
Tucker Brooke. New Haven: Yale University Press, 1925.

The Pelican Shakespeare, ed. Alfred Harbage. Baltimore:
Penguin Books, Inc., 1963.

BOOKS AND ARTICLES ABOUT *Love's Labor's Lost*

Barber, C. L. *Shakespeare's Festive Comedy*. Princeton, N. J.:
Princeton University Press, 1959.

Bradbrook, M. C. *The School of Night: a Study in the Literary Relationship of Sir Walter Raleigh*. Cambridge,
England: The University Press, 1936.

Campbell, O. J. "*Love's Labour's Lost* restudied," in *Michi-
gan Studies in Shakespeare, Milton and Donne* (New York,
1925), pp. 3–45.

Campbell, O. J. *Shakespeare's Satire*. London: Oxford University Press, 1943.

Charlton, H. B. *Shakespearian Comedy*. London: Methuen
and Co., Ltd., 1938.

Clark, E. L. *The Satirical Comedy of Love's Labour's Lost:
a study*. New York: Payson, 1933.

Frye, Northrop. "Shakespeare's Experimental Comedy," in *Stratford Papers on Shakespeare* (1961), pp. 2–14.

Gittings, Robert. *Shakespeare's Rival*. London: William Heinemann, Ltd., 1960.

Granville-Barker, Harley. "Love's Labour's Lost," in *Prefaces to Shakespeare*, Vol. IV. Princeton, N. J.: Princeton University Press, 1946. Paperback edition (1965).

Gray, Austin K. "The secret of *Love's Labour's Lost*," PMLA, XXXIX (1924), 581–611.

Gray, H. D. *The original version of Love's Labour's Lost*. Palo Alto, Cal.: Stanford University, 1918.

Harbage, Alfred. "*Love's Labour's Lost* and the Early Shakespeare," *Philological Quarterly*, XLI (1962), 18–36.

Hoy, Cyrus. "*Love's Labour's Lost* and the Nature of Comedy," *Shakespeare Quarterly*, XIII (1962), 31–40.

Lambrechts, G. " 'The brief and the tedious of it': Note sur le texte de *Love's Labour's Lost*," *Etudes Anglaises*, XVII (1964), 269–283.

Le Franc, Abel. *Sous le masque de Shakespeare*. 2 vols. (Paris, 1912).

Lever, J. W. "Three Notes on Shakespeare's Plants," *Review of English Studies*, III (1952), 117–120.

Nevinson, John L. "A Show of the Nine Worthies," *Shakespeare Quarterly*, XIV (1963), 103–107.

Oakeshott, Walter. *The Queen and the Poet*. London: Faber and Faber, Ltd., 1960.

Pater, Walter. "Love's Labour's Lost," in *Appreciations* (1889), pp. 167–175.

Schrickx, W. *Shakespeare's Early Contemporaries. The Background of the Harvey-Nashe Polemic and Love's Labour's Lost* (Antwerp, 1956).

Taylor, R. *The date of Love's Labour's Lost*. New York: Columbia University Press, 1932.

Traversi, Derek. *Shakespeare: The Early Comedies*. London: Longmans Green & Co., Ltd., 1960.

Tillyard, E. M. W. *Shakespeare's Early Comedies*. New York: Barnes & Noble, Inc., 1965.

Ungerer, Gustav. "Two Items of Spanish Pronunciation in

Love's Labour's Lost," *Shakespeare Quarterly,* XIV (1963), 245–251.

Westlund, Joseph. "Fancy and Achievement in *Love's Labour's Lost,*" *Shakespeare Quarterly,* XVIII (1967), 37–46.

Wilson, J. Dover. *Shakespeare's Happy Comedies.* Evanston, Ill.: Northwestern University Press, 1962.

Yates, F. A. *A Study of Love's Labour's Lost.* Cambridge, England: The University Press, 1936.